U.S. History
People and Events in African-American History

By
GEORGE LEE

COPYRIGHT © 2006 Mark Twain Media, Inc.

ISBN 1-58037-335-6

Printing No. CD-404038

Mark Twain Media, Inc., Publishers
Distributed by Carson-Dellosa Publishing Company, Inc.

Revised/Previously published as *Decisions and the African-American Experience: 1619–1993*

Table of Contents

Introduction iv

Time Line 1

A New Market for the Slave Trade 4

Las Casas in the West Indies 6

Slaves in the American Colonies. 8

The Middle Passage 10

Slavery as a Social and Legal System 12

Slavery in the American Revolution 14

Constitutional Compromises on Slavery 16

Some African-Americans Defy Stereotypes 18

The Cotton Gin and Slavery 20

Slaves Find Power in Religion 22

Northern African-Americans Form Separate Churches 24

African-Americans Oppose Colonization 26

The Missouri Compromise 28

Slaves Make a Life for Themselves 30

Slaves Rebel in Different Ways 32

The Abolition Movement 34

Slavery Debates in Congress 36

The Underground Railroad 38

Uncle Tom vs. Blackface Minstrels 40

The Battle Over Kansas 42

Courts, Debates, and Attacks 44

African-Americans Agitate for Freedom 46

African-Americans Fight for Freedom 48

The Road to Freedom 50

Reconstruction 52

From Slavery to Sharecropping 54

Cowboys, Exodusters, and Soldiers 56

African-Americans Head North 58

Table of Contents (cont.)

Booker T. Washington...60

The Disfranchising of African-Americans...62

"Separate but Equal"...64

Founding the NAACP...66

The Urban League...68

African-Americans in World War I..70

Postwar America...72

Marcus Garvey and Racial Pride...74

Ragtime, Jazz, and Blues...76

The New Deal..78

Jobs Created by World War II..80

African-Americans Fight in World War II...82

Truman Stands Up for Equality...84

The Landmark *Brown* Decision...86

Moving to the Front of the Bus...88

Desegregating Little Rock Central High...90

The Civil Rights Movement..92

Radical Movements..94

The Civil and Voting Rights Acts...96

Pain and Trouble in the Late 1960s...98

African-Americans Move to the City...100

Rising African-American Influence in Politics..102

Sports and Entertainment..104

Affirmative Action and Busing..106

Colin Powell: Top General and Diplomat..108

Condoleezza Rice: Political Powerhouse...110

Answer Keys...112

Bibliography/Suggestions for Further Reading...123

Introduction

When the author was in school in the late 1940s and early 1950s, many African-Americans and nearly all whites were unaware that African-Americans had any history worth studying. Except for a few familiar names like Booker T. Washington and George Washington Carver, African-Americans were not mentioned in textbooks, except as they affected white controversies. It was not until the civil rights movement was well underway that African-American history began to receive serious study. In 1969–70, I was fortunate enough to spend a year submerged in African-American history as a fellow at the Johns Hopkins University's Institute of Southern History. It was an eye-opening experience, and I was confronted by people and events in African-American history that I had never known before.

This book is about some of those people and the decisions that have shaped African-American history in the United States. These help us understand where we are as a nation and how we got here. On some topics, the reader may wish to do more research, and that is encouraged. Relevant websites are given in each chapter for students to use in researching the topics further. A list of references is also included in the back of the book.

The information in this book is correlated with the National Council of Social Studies (NCSS™) curriculum standards and the National Standards of History (NSH). It also supports the No Child Left Behind (NCLB) initiative.

The study of history is important because if we don't know where we have been, we have no way to understand the present or predict the future. We should not try to hide from the past, even the unpleasant parts, so the bad decisions that were made have been included along with those that brought achievement and growth. Progress for the individual, race, or nation depends on how *we* as individuals and groups evaluate our decisions and react to those of others. Wise decisions pull us up; foolish decisions push us down. As humans of any race, we are all capable of both wisdom and folly.

–The Author–

Time Line

A time line helps us understand the order in which events occurred. We use time lines all our lives. We say we were born in ＿＿ and started school in ＿＿. In ＿＿, we moved to ＿＿. They also help us keep historical events in sequence.

1472	Slave trade with Benin begins.
1492	Columbus sails to the New World.
1517	Slaves are first sent to the West Indies by Spain.
1607	Jamestown Colony is established in Virginia.
1619	African "bound servants" arrive in Jamestown.
1620	Plymouth Colony is established.
1630	Massachusetts Bay Colony is established.
1671	Maryland's Act of 1671 says an African-American's religious conversion does not change the status of a slave.
1672–98	The Royal African Company has a monopoly on the slave trade.
1712	New York City slave revolt occurs.
1732	Georgia, the last of the thirteen colonies, is established without slavery.
1739	South Carolina has three slave uprisings.
1755	Georgia passes a law permitting slavery.
1754–63	French and Indian War
1770	Crispus Attucks, an escaped slave, is killed in the Boston Massacre.
1773	Boston Tea Party
1776	Declaration of Independence declares that "all men are created equal."
1780–86	Gradual freeing of slaves begins in northern states.
1783	*Quok Walker* decision ends slavery in Massachusetts.
1787	Northwest Ordinance bars slavery in the Northwest Territories.
1787	Constitutional Convention approves Three-Fifths Compromise: slave trade for 20 more years and the return of fugitive slaves.
1793	Fugitive Slave Law is passed by Congress.
1793	The cotton gin is invented by Eli Whitney.
1800	Thomas Jefferson is elected president.
1800	Gabriel Prosser revolt takes place in Virginia.
1803	Louisiana Purchase
1804	Haiti declares independence from France.
1812–14	War of 1812
1816	American Colonization Society is formed.
1820	Missouri Compromise
1821	Benjamin Lundy's anti-slavery journal, *Genius of Universal Emancipation,* begins publication.
1821	Denmark Vesey's rebellion occurs in South Carolina.
1831	Nat Turner rebellion occurs in Virginia.
1831	William Lloyd Garrison's newspaper *The Liberator* is first published.
1833	American Anti-Slavery Society is formed.

Time Line (cont.)

1836	Texas War for Independence
1840	Liberty Party is formed.
1844	Methodist and Baptist Churches split over slavery.
1846	The Mexican War begins.
1846	Wilmot Proviso proposes to keep slavery out of any new lands taken from Mexico.
1848	The Mexican War ends.
1850	Compromise of 1850
1852	*Uncle Tom's Cabin* by Harriet Beecher Stowe is published.
1854	Kansas-Nebraska Bill is proposed and passed.
1857	*Dred Scott* decision
1859	John Brown's raid on Harpers Ferry
1860	Lincoln is elected; South Carolina secedes.
1862	Emancipation Proclamation is announced.
1863	U.S. African-American troops enlist in the Union Army. Slavery is abolished in the District of Columbia.
1865	The Civil War ends; Lincoln is assassinated and dies; Andrew Johnson is now president. The Thirteenth Amendment ends slavery. Black Codes are passed in the southern states.
1866	Civil Rights Act passes; Ku Klux Klan is formed.
1867	Reconstruction Act passes; Freedmen's Bureau ends.
1868	The Fourteenth Amendment is ratified.
1870s–80s	Exodusters go to Kansas.
1877	End of Reconstruction
1881	Tuskegee Institute is chartered.
1888	Colored Farmers' Alliance is formed.
1890	Afro-American League is formed to fight discrimination.
1890s	Jim Crow laws are passed in the South.
1895	Atlanta Compromise speech is given by Booker T. Washington.
1896	*Plessy v. Ferguson* decision by the Supreme Court
1898	Spanish-American War
1901	Booker T. Washington is invited to lunch at the White House.
1906	Brownsville (Texas) riot
1910	The NAACP is formed.
1911	National Urban League is formed.
1912	Woodrow Wilson is elected president.
1914	World War I begins in Europe; UNIA is formed by Marcus Garvey.
1915	*Birth of a Nation* is the first full-length movie; Ku Klux Klan is reborn.
1917	The United States enters World War I; Emmett Scott is named as advisor.
1919	Race riots spread across the nation; Black Star Line is started by Marcus Garvey.
1925	*The New Negro* (Alain Locke) and *Home To Harlem* (Claude McKay) are published.
1929	Stock market crash begins the Great Depression.
1931	Scottsboro Trial; retrial of those convicted is ordered by the Supreme Court in 1933.

Time Line (cont.)

1932	Franklin D. Roosevelt is elected president.
1933	Black Cabinet is formed; New Deal programs hire African-Americans.
1939	World War II breaks out.
1941	March on Washington is called off by A. Philip Randolph; Executive Order 8802 is issued by President Franklin D. Roosevelt; United States enters World War II.
1942	The navy allows African-Americans to enlist.
1943	Race riots occur in Detroit and other cities.
1945	World War II ends.
1947	Jackie Robinson is the first African-American major league baseball player.
1948	Dixiecrats break with the Democratic party.
1951	Army desegregation begins.
1954	*Brown v. Board of Education* decision attacks segregation.
1956	Montgomery bus boycott is led by Martin Luther King, Jr.
1957	Little Rock desegregation battle takes place at Central High School.
1960	SNCC is formed; Civil Rights Act of 1960 is passed by Congress.
1961	Freedom rides protest segregation in transportation.
1962	James Meredith is admitted to the University of Mississippi.
1963	Martin Luther King, Jr., is arrested in Birmingham. Civil Rights March on Washington, D.C.
1964	Civil Rights Act of 1964 is passed by Congress.
1965	Malcolm X is assassinated; Voting Rights Act is passed by Congress; Watts riot takes place in Los Angeles.
1966	Black Panthers are organized.
1967	Thurgood Marshall is appointed to the Supreme Court.
1968	Martin Luther King, Jr., is assassinated.
1971–75	Major busing controversy
1972	Supreme Court nominees Clement Haynesworth and G. Harold Carswell are not confirmed because of strong African-American opposition.
1978	*Bakke* decision bars racial quotas.
1987	Colin Powell is the first African-American National Security Advisor; he becomes the first African-American Chairman of the Joint Chiefs of Staff (1989).
1992	Los Angeles riots after police officers are acquitted in the Rodney King beating case.
2001	Colin Powell is named Secretary of State; Condoleezza Rice is named National Security Advisor.
2005	Condoleezza Rice becomes Secretary of State; U.S. Senate passes a resolution apologizing for not outlawing lynchings in the past.

A New Market for the Slave Trade

Askia Muhammed Ture

Across the savanna grasslands south of the Sahara, travelers had come to settle or trade for centuries. First to arrive were the Bantu, settling in about 1000 B.C. At times they flourished, as they farmed, developed iron technology, and created powerful kingdoms. Although separated from the northern Mediterranean by the Sahara Desert, they were never completely isolated. Arab camel caravans brought in salt and copper and went home with cargoes of gold, ivory, and slaves.

Cities existed, but most of the people lived in small villages, where they farmed without the benefit of plows or draft animals. Villagers often could not communicate with their neighbors: 264 different languages existed in the Sudan and 182 among the Bantu. With no written language, traditions had to be memorized. Family lines were based on the mother's side, but as wars and economic changes occurred, by the 15th century, the husband was growing in importance.

The first kingdom south of the Sahara, Ghana, was ruled by the Soninke dynasty, and an Arab traveler reported in 1067 that some of Ghana's large 200,000-man army wore chain mail. Gold was the main source of the king's wealth, and his dogs wore gold collars. Ghana's end came in 1203, and a rival, Mali, became the new power of West Africa. Located south and east of Ghana, Mali, at its height during the reign of Mansa Musa, had a population of 40 million. In 1384, Musa demonstrated his wealth as he traveled to Mecca accompanied by thousands of servants and soldiers. Realizing the importance of education, he brought Arab scholars to Timbuktu, and for a time, it was the most important center of learning in the world.

Holding Mali together was too much for Musa's successors, and Sonni Ali, ruler of Songhai, rose to challenge and defeat them. Ali's successor, Askia Muhammed Ture, ruled from 1493 to 1528 with a highly organized government. Defeat by Moroccans in 1591 ended the power and glory of Songhai.

The commercial center of Benin, located in the southern part of present Nigeria, was ruled by Obas (kings) through a council of family members, and the royal family's ties to local villages were through chiefs all related to the Oba. An active slave trade with Arabs provided Benin with guns and gunpowder. The king lived in a magnificent palace and was surrounded by priests, servants, and a harem of 1,000 wives.

In 1472, a Portuguese ship captain came to Benin, bowed before the Oba, and told him that he wanted to trade ivory, gold, and slaves. The Oba, with his arms covered in gold, gave his approval.

Across West Africa, other slave traders would soon be buying slaves. English and Dutch, as well as Portuguese, were bribing, persuading, or intimidating rulers. The rulers were either scared by the threats or lured by the gifts of guns, ammunition, and presents offered by the Europeans.

RESULTS: The Arab slave traders found a strong European competition developing, and neither side was above supplying arms to help one tribe against another. No strong kingdoms hindered the new slave trade, and no wise rulers united them. The villagers of West Africa paid the price.

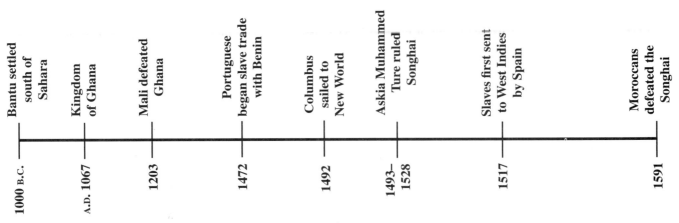

Bantu settled south of Sahara	Kingdom of Ghana	Mali defeated Ghana	Portuguese began slave trade with Benin	Columbus sailed to New World	Askia Muhammed Ture ruled Songhai	Slaves first sent to West Indies by Spain	Moroccans defeated the Songhai
1000 B.C.	A.D. 1067	1203	1472	1492	1493–1528	1517	1591

Name: _____ Date: _____

A New Market for the Slave Trade: Reinforcement

Directions: Complete the following activities, essays, and challenges on your own paper.

ACTIVITIES:

1. Create a map showing the locations of ancient kingdoms of West Africa.
2. Discuss what the class thinks rulers of West Africa must have been thinking when travelers came offering them guns in exchange for slaves.

ESSAYS:

1. If someone were to tell you that Africans were savages before slave traders came, how would you answer them?
2. What problems did rulers have in trying to build kingdoms in West Africa?
3. If you were able to speak with the Oba, what would you ask or tell him?

CHALLENGES:

1. When did the Bantu first arrive in the area south of the Sahara Desert?
2. What did the Bantu buy from the Arabs; what did they sell?
3. How many languages were spoken in the Sudan? Among the Bantu?
4. What was the first kingdom south of the Sahara, and what family ruled it?
5. Where was Mali located? Who was its most powerful ruler?
6. What city became the center of learning in Mali?
7. What two rulers were especially important in Songhai history?
8. What was the ruler of Benin called? How did he control his country?
9. From where was the ship captain who approached the Oba of Benin, and what did he want to trade?
10. Which European nations were involved in the slave trade?

NATIONAL STANDARDS CORRELATIONS:

NCSS VIf: (Power, Authority, & Governance) Explain conditions, actions, and motivations that contribute to conflict and cooperation within and among nations.
NSH Era 1, Standard 1: Comparative characteristics of societies in the Americas, Western Europe, and Western Africa that increasingly interacted after 1450

WEBSITES:

http://web.cocc.edu/cagatucci/classes/hum211/timelines/htimeline3.htm
"Part III: African Slave Trade & European Imperialism: AD/CE 15th–early 19th centuries," Central Oregon Community College

http://www.cnmat.berkeley.edu/~ladzekpo/maps.html
"Maps of Africa and Ghana," University of California, Berkeley

http://www.wsu.edu:8080/~dee/CIVAFRCA/FOREST.HTM
"Civilizations in Africa: the forest kingdoms," Washington State University

Las Casas in the West Indies

Bartolomé de Las Casas, as a young man in Seville, had seen Columbus return to the city and had watched his father leave with Columbus on his second voyage. After studying theology and fighting Moors with the militia, Las Casas sailed to the New World in 1502 and was given an estate *(encomienda),* which gave him the power to work the natives on his land. In 1506, he gave up his land, went to Rome, and became a priest. In 1512, he returned, and the next year he received another *encomienda.* Like another priest, Antonio de Montesinos, who had attacked the *encomiendas* in Santo Domingo, Las Casas became appalled by the cruel treatment the peaceful, gentle natives suffered.

To their Spanish conquerors, these natives were savages: pagan, naked, lazy, idol worshipers. King Ferdinand ruled that the natives must acknowledge him as their ruler and accept his religion, or they would be enslaved. When these instructions were read to them in Spanish and Latin, the natives ignored them and suffered the consequences. Realizing that the natives faced extermination unless another source of labor could be found, Las Casas returned to Spain with a new proposal.

Bartolomé de Las Casas

Some Africans had already been shipped to the colonies to work in the sugar fields, and they were surviving the hard work in the terrible heat. His plan was simple: replace natives with African workers. King Ferdinand gave his approval, and in 1517, he issued the first *asiento* (permit to import slaves). Later in life, Las Casas realized he had made a tragic mistake, but it was much too late to stop the profitable slave traffic that had begun as a result. While the Portuguese were the first to enter the trade, they soon had strong competition from English and Dutch traders—the best-known was Sir John Hawkins. Forts and "factories" (holding areas for slaves) dotted the African coastline.

Slaves accompanied the major Spanish conquerors: Balboa, Cortés, Pizarro, and Narvaez. Of the four survivors of the Narvaez expedition, Estevanico was one. Surviving eight years among the Native Americans, he had heard stories of the Seven Cities of Gold. In 1539, he served as scout for Fray Marcos's expedition. Moving too far in advance of the party, he was murdered by the Native Americans. Marcos returned to Mexico, and the following year, Coronado led an ill-fated party through the American southwest.

South of the Caribbean region lay Portuguese Brazil, which brought in Bantus, Sudanese, Kaffirs, Hottentots, and Bushmen as slaves. Some argue that Brazilian slavery was easier for the Africans, and that it was easy for them to adjust to the milder climate. However, it is clear that the slaves did most of the work and, at times, were victims of cruel treatment. Some escaped into the interior and formed colonies *(quilombos)* where they governed themselves. The most noted of these was in northeast Brazil and was called Palmarea; it was a haven for runaway slaves from 1630 to 1697.

RESULTS: Slaves were brought to the New World to do the work natives could not do and the Spanish and Portuguese refused to do. Their earlier example would be followed by the English settling North America.

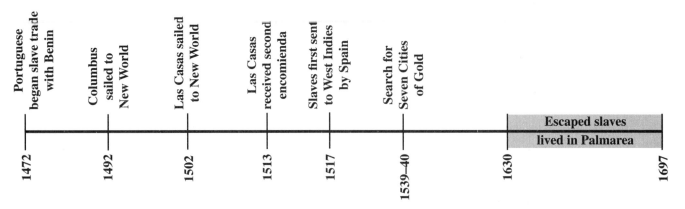

Portuguese began slave trade with Benin	Columbus sailed to New World	Las Casas sailed to New World	Las Casas received second encomienda	Slaves first sent to West Indies by Spain	Search for Seven Cities of Gold	Escaped slaves lived in Palmarea
1472	1492	1502	1513	1517	1539–40	1630 — 1697

Name: _____ Date: _____

Las Casas in the West Indies: Reinforcement

Directions: Complete the following activities, essays, and challenges on your own paper.

ACTIVITIES:

1. Discuss the question of Las Casas' request to bring in African slaves. What were the alternatives available? Did he choose the right one?
2. Discuss the attitudes that Europeans must have had to justify what they did to Native Americans and African slaves.

ESSAYS:

1. As a Native American in the West Indies, how would your view of Las Casas differ from that of an African?
2. Why do you think King Ferdinand took the attitude he did toward the Native Americans and toward the Africans?
3. Many slave colonies were established in Brazil, but very few in the West Indies. How would you explain that?

CHALLENGES:

1. What was an *encomienda?*
2. What profession did Las Casas choose?
3. What priest on Santo Domingo attacked the encomiendas?
4. Why did the Spanish feel that they did not have to treat the Native Americans like humans?
5. Why did the natives refuse to accept Ferdinand as their king?
6. Why did Las Casas suggest bringing in African slaves?
7. What was the permit to import slaves called?
8. What were "factories"?
9. Who was the scout for Marcos's expedition to find the "Seven Cities of Gold"?
10. What were *quilombos?* What was the most famous one, and how long did it survive?

NATIONAL STANDARDS CORRELATIONS:

NCSS Ve: (Individuals, Groups, & Institutions) Identify and describe examples of tensions between belief systems and government policies and laws.
NSH Era 1, Standard 2: How early European exploration and colonization resulted in cultural and ecological interactions among previously unconnected peoples

WEBSITES:

http://historicaltextarchive.com/sections.php?op=viewarticle&artid=444
"Las Casas, Man Who Made a Difference," Historical Text Archive

http://www.digitalhistory.uh.edu/learning_history/spain/spain_delascasas.cfm
"Bartolomé de las Casas (1542)," Digital History

http://chnm.gmu.edu/revolution/d/569/
"The Slaves from Africa," George Mason University and City University of New York

Slaves in the American Colonies

Social and economic institutions are often born of necessity, and it is not until later that rules and justifications develop. When societies look at labor that must be done, they often turn the most unpopular jobs over to those who have no choice except to do them. These jobs do not have to be difficult or demeaning. The Romans, for example, used slaves as policemen, bank managers, ship captains, and farm managers. In medieval times, whether labeled serfs, peasants, villeins, or slaves, a large underclass worked with little reward for Europe's royalty, nobility, and merchants.

Africans, too, were accustomed to slavery, and they were used for many purposes: soldiers, caravan workers, and royal officials, as well as menial laborers. While slaves could be sold, their children could not, so they sometimes became part of the master's family or were freed. As selling slaves to Arabs and Europeans became more profitable, African rulers appointed *caboceer* as agents to deal with slave traders.

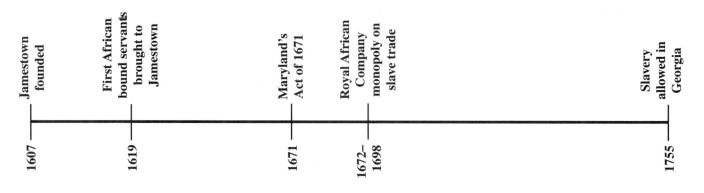

Annapolis, Sept. 29, 1767.
JUST IMPORTED,
In the Ship Lord Ligonier, Capt. DAVIES, from the River Gambia, in Africa, and to be fold by the Subfcribers, in Annapolis, for Cafh, or good Bills of Exchange, on Wednefday the 7th of October next,
A Cargo of choice healthy SLAVES. The faid Ship will take TOBACCO to London, on Liberty, at 6l. Sterling per Ton.
JOHN RIDOUT,
DANIEL of St. Thos. JENIFER.

Advertisement for sale of slaves

The English who established colonies were interested in finding workers to do hard labor. Their previous experience with this came when their armies established estates (plantations) in Ireland's northern counties. Henry VIII told the planters that he did not wish to destroy the Irish, but he did intend that they become obedient to his laws, forsake their old habits and customs, and teach their children the English language. The English saw the Irish as barely human savages, using similar descriptions to those used later to describe Native Americans and Africans.

The London Company, which had established the Virginia colony at Jamestown in 1607, was dissatisfied with its slow growth. By the end of 1618, the colony had barely 1,000 settlers. To increase the labor force, the company sent 100 poor children as "bound apprentices" to the colony. The Virginians found another source of workers. In August 1619 John Rolfe recorded the arrival of "a Dutch man of warre that sold us twenty Negars." These and the small number of servants who followed were listed as "bound servants" and, like white servants, were apparently freed at the end of their service. One enterprising African-American, Anthony Johnson, came as a servant in 1622 but was himself an importer of white and African indentured servants by 1651.

Marylanders needed workers as well, but they avoided using slave laborers because if the slaves converted to Christianity, they might be freed. The Act of 1671 said a slave's religion did not affect his status, so more slaves were sold in the colony. South Carolinians had no qualms about using slaves, but businessmen feared that so many would come that prices would fall. Georgia's founder, James Oglethorpe, intended that the colony's land should be reserved for English debtors; but when they saw other colonies growing more wealthy, slavery came to Georgia in 1755. Northern colonists preferred white indentured servants, and African-Americans were never more than two percent of the population.

RESULTS: The Southern Colonies used African servants and slaves to improve their economic well-being. While they were simply interested in getting work done, they were also beginning a social institution.

Jamestown founded	First African bound servants brought to Jamestown	Maryland's Act of 1671	Royal African Company monopoly on slave trade	Slavery allowed in Georgia
1607	1619	1671	1672–1698	1755

Name: _____ Date: _____

Slaves in the American Colonies: Reinforcement

Directions: Complete the following activities, essays, and challenges on your own paper.

ACTIVITIES:

1. Define the terms *peasant*, *villein*, and *serf* and compare their definitions with the term *slave*.
2. Ask the class what the "underclass" jobs are today that are often taken by minorities in the United States. Then ask what the difference is between those workers and slave laborers.

ESSAYS:

1. Why was slavery not the same everywhere in the world?
2. Do you think that the Irish example given in the reading was what was later expected of slaves as well?
3. Do you think that the "bound servants," or those Virginians who bought them, had any idea that they were doing anything unusual or important?

CHALLENGES:

1. Who used slaves as policemen and ship captains?
2. What terms were used in European nations to refer to the underclass who did the hard work?
3. What uses, besides as menial laborers, did Africans have for slaves?
4. Who were the *caboceer?*
5. Who ordered that the Irish must learn obedience, English customs, and the English language?
6. What did the London Company do to increase Jamestown's population?
7. From whom did the settlers at Jamestown buy their first Africans?
8. What designation was given to the 20 Africans sold in 1619?
9. What concern did South Carolinians have about importing slaves?
10. Why was James Oglethorpe opposed to bringing slaves to Georgia?

NATIONAL STANDARDS CORRELATIONS:

NCSS VIIf: (Production, Distribution, & Consumption) Explain and illustrate how values and beliefs influence different economic decisions.
NSH Era 2, Standard 1: Why the Americas attracted Europeans, why they brought enslaved Africans to their colonies, and how Europeans struggled for control of North America and the Caribbean

WEBSITES:

http://www.pbs.org/wgbh/aia/part1/narrative.html
"Africans in America," Public Broadcasting Service

http://www.history.org/Almanack/people/african/aaintro.cfm
"Introduction to Colonial African-American Life," The Colonial Williamsburg Foundation

http://www.historypoint.org/education/teaching/history_backyard/tobacco_slavery_virginia_colonies.asp
"Tobacco and Slavery in the Virginia Colony," Central Rappahannock Regional Library

The Middle Passage

Imagine yourself walking alone one day, and you are kidnapped; a rope is placed around your neck, and you are taken away to a big fort where you are tossed in with total strangers. Given barely enough food to survive, and with all dignity removed, you spend weeks wondering when you will die. One day a strange-looking man walks in, looks you over, decides that "you'll do," and takes you to a ship. Aboard the ship are many other prisoners who, like you, are terrified and hoping to find someone they know.

'Tween decks area of a slaver

You have just entered the "middle passage." The slaver (slave ship) on which you are sailing may have begun its voyage in Boston or Providence, carrying cloth, guns, or rum to Africa. After delivering its cargo of slaves to the West Indies or the South, it will take sugar or cotton back to Boston, the third leg of its trip. The ship on which you sail is average for the trade. You are crowded in the 'tween decks section (between the deck and the hold). On most 18th-century slavers, the 'tween decks is only 3'10" high, and the average space for each slave was 16" wide and 5.5' long. The crew sleeps on the deck. Food and water are stored below. The portholes are closed and bolted to prevent slaves from jumping overboard. The heat is stifling, and many on board are seasick. You are taken to the deck once or twice a day to be fed. A pasty substance, gruel, is given to you in a dipper.

It is little consolation to know that the crew is often as sick as you are, and that a higher percentage of them may die than the slaves on the voyage. Common diseases like yellow fever, dysentery, and malaria have little effect on the Africans but are fatal to the crews. Drinking stagnant water and eating the stale food make this a dangerous business for the crew as well as the passengers. Callous captains overload the slavers, expecting a high attrition. Slaves unable to communicate with each other and weak with hunger usually offer little resistance. The last two or three days at sea are often the best. Food and water rations are increased so the slaves will look healthier and bring a better price.

Despite the feeble condition of the passengers and a lack of a common language, there are times when the slaves revolt. The usual rebellion is by giving up and dying, either through self-starvation or jumping overboard. To prevent slaves from starving themselves, a funnel is heated and pressed against their lips; when the lips open, food is poured in. The crew will grab anyone attempting to jump. Many simply quit living (suicidal melancholy), and their bodies are tossed overboard to the sharks. There are 55 documented occasions when slaves revolted and hundreds of references to others. A good example was when the undermanned crew of the *Perfect* was overwhelmed by slaves in 1759. After running the ship ashore, they looted and burned it.

RESULTS: Statistics on the loss of life during middle passage are only fragmentary, but they suggest that the terrible reputation of the business was deserved. Some captains did try to make the trip safe and provided for the health of the slaves, but most were interested only in profit and were not interested in providing any type of humane treatment for the slaves.

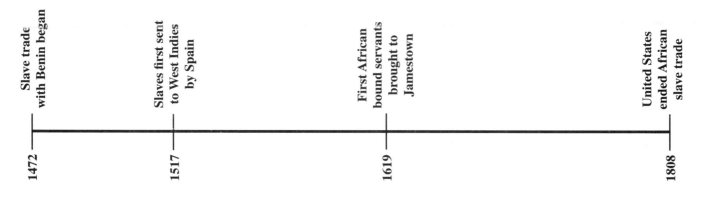

Slave trade with Benin began — 1472

Slaves first sent to West Indies by Spain — 1517

First African bound servants brought to Jamestown — 1619

United States ended African slave trade — 1808

Name: _____ Date: _____

The Middle Passage: Reinforcement

Directions: Complete the following activities, essays, and challenges on your own paper.

ACTIVITIES:

1. As described in the reading, measure off the right amount of "slave space" for each student, and have them lie in it on the floor. Make an "entrance" that is 3′10″ high, and ask each student to walk through and keep his or her head below it.
2. Discuss the question: After an experience like middle passage, which might last six months, would home seem as clear in your memory after it was over?

ESSAYS:

1. As a crew member on a slaver, discuss the conditions on board the ship, and explain why you are in the business.
2. As a slave 'tween decks, what would you try to think about, and how would you feel about your fellow prisoners and the crew?
3. As the owner of a slaver, how much guilt would you bear when conditions on board your ship are so bad? How do you answer your critics?

CHALLENGES:

1. What goods were carried from New England to Africa?
2. What was the name given to the cargo area reserved for slaves, and where on the ship was it located?
3. How much width, length, and height was there allotted to each slave on a slaver?
4. In spite of the heat, why were portholes closed?
5. What diseases were especially hard on slaver crews?
6. Why weren't slave revolts common on every voyage?
7. How did conditions improve in the last two or three days of a voyage, and why?
8. When a slave refused food, how did the crew make him eat?
9. How many documented revolts occurred on slavers, and how many references were there to others?
10. What happened when the slaves on the *Perfect* took over the ship?

NATIONAL STANDARDS CORRELATIONS:

NCSS IIe: (Time, Continuity, & Change) Develop critical sensitivities such as empathy and skepticism regarding attitudes, values, and behaviors of people in different historical contexts.
NSH Era 2, Standard 3: How the values and institutions of European economic life took root in the colonies, and how slavery reshaped European and African life in the Americas

WEBSITES:

http://www.melfisher.org/henriettamarie/middlepassage/htm
"The Wreck of the *Henrietta Marie*: Introduction," Mel Fisher Maritime Heritage Society, Inc.

http://www.juneteenth.com/middlep.htm
"The Middle Passage," Tom Feelings

http://www.eyewitnesstohistory.com/slaveship.htm
"Aboard a Slave Ship, 1829," Eyewitness to History

Slavery as a Social and Legal System

The English colonists of North America knew they needed helpers to build their homes and work in them. They also needed help to plow and harvest their land. There were a variety of sources of this labor. *Indentured servants* gave four to seven years of labor just to pay for their transportation to America. *Apprentices* were orphans or children of poor parents who were given to a farmer or tradesman to be trained; they would be freed when they reached a specified age. *Convicts* were released from English prisons and sent to America; from 1750 to 1770, 10,000 were sent to Maryland alone. Eventually, many of these servants became fully accepted citizens of the colony.

Slave Auction

Having had no experience with slavery, North American colonists moved cautiously. First, Africans were "bound servants," then "servants for life," and eventually, they were "slaves." Few Africans came to North America before the 1660s; most were being sent to Brazil and the West Indies. Virginia had only 300 African servants in 1650. However, three important changes occurred to increase the numbers.

First, the Company of Royal Adventurers was formed in 1663 and was to supply a minimum of 3,000 slaves annually to the American colonists. Led by the Duke of York, brother of the king of England, it was so influential that a new coin for the African slave trade was struck. Called the "guinea," its value equaled the pound sterling. Not only did these slave traders have money, but they had high connections.

Second, the overproduction of sugar in the West Indies resulted in soil depletion. As crops dropped and a demand for slaves increased on the mainland, West Indian planters sold off surplus workers to Americans.

Third, a higher percentage of female slaves came to North America than to the West Indies and Brazil. This increased the percentage of slaves who were American born. Owners could see obvious possibilities of workers replacing workers through natural means, and they encouraged slave marriages.

The increase in numbers and the changing status from "bound servant" to "slave" required that new laws be written. For example, did *conversion to Christianity* free them from slavery? Maryland's Act of 1671 said it did not. Was the *punishment for crime* the same for a slave as a free man? Virginia put much tougher penalties on slaves for committing crimes than it did on whites. When a *child was born*, did it receive the status of the father or mother? Colonists ruled that it was the mother's child and inherited her status of slave. How should *slave revolts* be discouraged? South Carolina allowed any white to search any slave for offensive weapons. Should slaves be allowed to *congregate?* Georgia said that no more than seven could be present at one place, unless a white was with them. On the question of whether slaves should be allowed to *read and write,* Georgia said they must not. Could slaves *testify* in a trial where the defendant was white? New York said no.

RESULTS: Slavery did not begin with a single flourish of a pen. It slowly began to take form, with one colony borrowing rules and regulations from others. It was never quite uniform, but it could be said that it was never equal or just in its treatment of slaves accused of any crime.

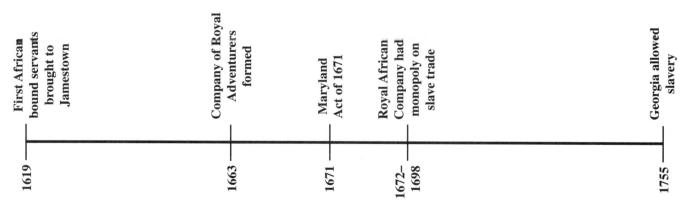

First African bound servants brought to Jamestown — 1619

Company of Royal Adventurers formed — 1663

Maryland Act of 1671 — 1671

Royal African Company had monopoly on slave trade — 1672–1698

Georgia allowed slavery — 1755

Name: _____ Date: _____

Slavery as a Social and Legal System: Reinforcement

Directions: Complete the following activities, essays, and challenges on your own paper.

ACTIVITIES:

1. Have three students discuss how they came to America (indentured, convict, slave) and how they feel about their situation now.
2. Have the students write rules and regulations restricting students in another grade.

ESSAYS:

1. Why were Marylanders reluctant to buy slaves until the question of slave conversions was cleared up?
2. If you were a colonial farmer, would you prefer to use an indentured servant or a slave? Why?
3. As a slave, which colony's rules would seem most unfair to you? Why?

CHALLENGES:

1. Why did people voluntarily give up freedom by becoming indentured servants?
2. Who were apprentices?
3. How many convicts were sent to Maryland in a 20-year period?
4. What was the connection between the Company of Royal Adventurers and royalty?
5. Why did West Indian planters start sending slaves to the mainland?
6. Why did owners encourage slave marriages?
7. What did Maryland rule in cases involving slave conversions to Christianity?
8. When a child was born to a slave woman, was the child legally the father's or the mother's?
9. In Georgia, what was the rule on slaves congregating in one place?
10. Were slaves allowed to testify against a white in New York?

NATIONAL STANDARDS CORRELATIONS:

NCSS Xa: (Civic Ideals & Practices) Examine the origins and continuing influence of key ideals of the democratic republican form of government, such as individual human dignity, liberty, justice, equality, and the rule of law.
NSH Era 2, Standard 3: How the values and institutions of European economic life took root in the colonies, and how slavery reshaped European and African life in the Americas

WEBSITES:

http://www.pbs.org/wnet/slavery/index.html
"Slavery and the Making of America," Public Broadcasting Service

http://www.nps.gov/hamp/lancaster1.htm
"Almost Chattel: The Lives of Indentured Servants at Hampton-Northampton, Baltimore County," National Park Service

http://earlyamerica.com/review/winter96/slavery.html
"Securing the Leg Irons: Restriction of Legal Rights for Slaves in Virginia and Maryland, 1625–1791," Archiving Early America

Slavery in the American Revolution

Battle of Bunker Hill

To slaves, the friction between England and the American colonists must have produced some interesting discussions. Patrick Henry's famous statement, "Is life so sweet as to be purchased at the price of chains and slavery? ... Give me liberty or give me death," may have seemed ironic. But the most curious statements of all belonged to slave-owning Thomas Jefferson. In his "Summary View," he said that the reason for the continued presence of the African slave trade was England's refusal to end it. In the Declaration of Independence, he penned the famous words: "All men are created equal," and among their inalienable rights were "life, liberty, and the pursuit of happiness." These words may have offered hope that things were about to change, but it was false hope to those enslaved in the South.

When fighting started, some African-Americans were caught up in revolutionary fervor. At Bunker Hill (actually Breed's Hill), slaves and free African-Americans participated, and Salem Poor was praised by his superiors as "an excellent soldier." When Washington took command, he told recruiters not to enlist African-Americans, but some were already in the army. In October 1775, it was decided to bar African-Americans from the Continental Army.

A month later, Governor Dunmore of Virginia declared that any slave or indentured servant who joined the British army would be free. Slaves began deserting the plantations and enlisting in the Royal Army. Wherever the British army went, slaves flocked in. The seriousness of his mistake was made apparent to Washington when many of his own slaves escaped.

Wisely reversing policy, Washington ordered in December 1775 that free African-Americans would be allowed to enlist in the Continental Army, and most states permitted both slave and free African-American enlistment in their militia. Massachusetts and Rhode Island had enough African-American volunteers to form separate regiments for them, but in many militia units, African-American soldiers served with whites. New York allowed freedom to any slave serving for three years. Two states, Georgia and South Carolina, refused to enlist African-American troops; but even in those states, slaves were leaving plantations to serve on one side or the other.

African-American soldiers participated in every major battle from Bunker Hill to Yorktown. They also served in the U.S. Navy. One of these was James Forten, who enlisted at 14 years old as a powder boy. After he was captured, he refused to leave with the English. He would later become a distinguished businessman, religious leader, and abolitionist.

The Quakers, who had protested slavery since the 17th century on religious grounds, were joined by others who opposed it for ethical reasons. John Jay, Ben Franklin, and Benjamin Rush were prominent citizens urging an end to slavery. Northern states started the process of abolishing slavery, and southern states passed laws making it easier to free slaves.

RESULTS: Both Patrick Henry's and Thomas Jefferson's dramatic statements about freedom may have been motivated by a desire to arouse anti-British emotions, but they also established a nobility of purpose that made slavery seem to be a violation of inalienable rights held by all of humanity.

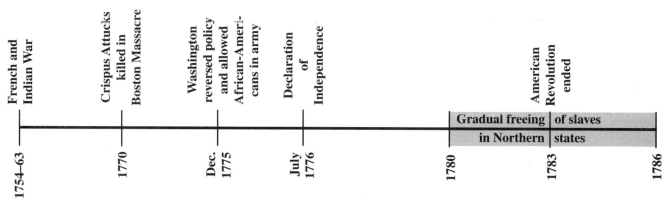

Name: _____ Date: _____

Slavery in the American Revolution: Reinforcement

Directions: Complete the following activities, essays, and challenges on your own paper.

ACTIVITIES:

1. Stage a discussion in the slave quarters, with two students arguing over whether they should escape to British lines.
2. Discuss how the class thinks the attitude of a white soldier might have been affected by having an African-American soldier fighting by his side.

ESSAYS:

1. If you had been a slave at the time of the Revolution, would you have accepted Lord Dunmore's invitation to escape? Why or why not?
2. As a slave first listening to the Declaration of Independence being read, what thoughts might have gone through your mind?
3. Why do you think the American Revolution was important to African-Americans?

CHALLENGES:

1. What issue concerning slavery was attacked in "Summary View"?
2. What were the "inalienable rights" mentioned in the Declaration of Independence?
3. Which African-American soldier distinguished himself at Bunker (Breed's) Hill?
4. Who encouraged slaves to join the English side?
5. What state offered freedom to slaves serving three years?
6. Which states refused to recruit African-American militiamen?
7. Which states had the largest numbers of African-American volunteers?
8. Who was the most famous African-American sailor in the Revolution?
9. Who were three prominent citizens who spoke out against slavery?
10. How did northern states differ from southern states in their solutions to end slavery?

NATIONAL STANDARDS CORRELATIONS:

NCSS Xc: (Civil Ideals & Practices) Locate, access, analyze, organize, and apply information about selected public issues—recognizing and explaining multiple points of view.

NSH Era 3, Standard 1: The causes of the American Revolution, the ideas and interests involved in forging the revolutionary movement, and the reasons for the American victory

WEBSITES:

http://docsouth.unc.edu/nell/html
"The Colored Patriots of the American Revolution, with Sketches of Several Distinguished Colored Persons," The University of North Carolina at Chapel Hill

http://www.pbs.org/wgbh/aia/part2/2narr4.html
"Africans in America: The Revolutionary War," Public Broadcasting Service

http://earlyamerica.com/review/2003_winter_spring/slavery_liberty.htm
"Slavery and Liberty in the American Revolution: John Lauren's Black Regiment Proposal," Archiving Early America

Constitutional Compromises on Slavery

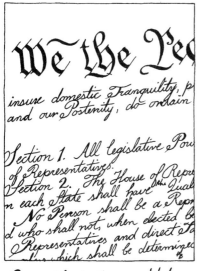

Preamble to the Constitution

The mood of the country had changed since the Revolution. The liberalism of 1776, which had led to the freeing of northern slaves and easing the freeing of southern slaves, had disappeared. The Confederation had failed to keep public confidence. Debtor riots in the North had required that the militia be called out to restore public order. Leaders worried about the dangers of foreign intrigue, rivalry between states, and the threat of King Mob. Idealism seemed less important now than stability and order.

The delegates meeting at Philadelphia in 1787 faced many troubling issues. The states they represented varied from large to small populations, from commercial to agricultural economies, from conservative to liberal philosophies, and from states recently abolishing slavery to states with no intention of ever ending it. Delegates knew that selection to this convention was more than just an honor; it was the most important opportunity they would ever have to make history. Failure meant the possible collapse of the United States. No issue, including slavery, was worth running the risk of going home without a new form of union.

The Confederation Congress had recently discussed slavery and had concluded in the Northwest Ordinance that slavery should not exist in territories north of the Ohio River. At the same time, Congress voted that any fugitive slave escaping to the region could be reclaimed by the master.

In Philadelphia, the Constitutional Convention could hardly dodge the questions that slavery raised. In regard to *taxation* and *representation,* especially, feelings ran hot. The South feared that a poll tax might be levied and slaves would be counted as persons for taxation purposes. When representation was discussed, the North opposed counting slaves at all. A compromise was reached that for both taxation and representation, "all other persons" [slaves] would count as three-fifths of a person.

The North wanted to end the *African slave trade.* Most delegates from the upper South agreed, because they had all the slaves they needed. However, South Carolina and Georgia needed more slaves and wanted to import more. A compromise was reached allowing the trade to continue another 20 years.

There was almost no discussion on the question of whether *fugitive slaves* were to be returned if they crossed state lines. Article IV, Section 2, said that any person escaping labor or service in one state and fleeing to another "shall be delivered up on claim of the party to whom such service or labor shall be due."

RESULTS: The Constitution was sent to the states for ratification and was adopted. Most would later praise it for creating an ingenious system of checks and balances, separation of powers, and limits on governmental power, but abolitionists saw it as a "compromise with hell" for refusing to take a hard stand on the slavery question.

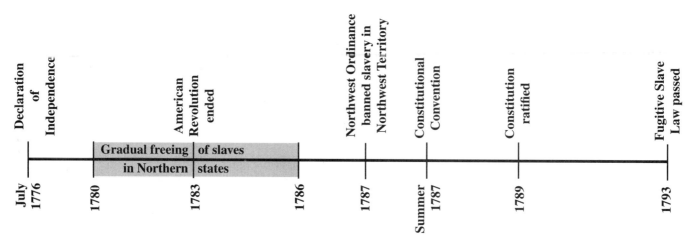

Name: _____ Date: _____

Constitutional Compromises on Slavery: Reinforcement

Directions: Complete the following activities, essays, and challenges on your own paper.

ACTIVITIES:

1. Have the class look up clauses in the Constitution relating to slaves.
2. Ask the class what changes *they* would have made in regard to slavery if they had been at the Convention.

ESSAYS:

1. The writers of the Constitution never mentioned "slaves" or "slavery," but used terms like "other persons," "persons held to service or labor," and "such persons." Why do you think they did this?
2. Why do you think that the Three-Fifths Compromise was acceptable to both North and South? Do you think there was any logical reason for that figure?
3. Remembering that the North had indentured servants and convict laborers, do you think they had any part in requiring the return of fugitives?

CHALLENGES:

1. What problems worried national leaders in 1787?
2. Why was slavery not high on the agenda at the Constitutional Convention?
3. What did the Northwest Ordinance do to limit slavery?
4. If a fugitive slave escaped to the Northwest Territories, what did the Ordinance require?
5. What did the South fear that the Convention might do that would harm their interests?
6. How did the North feel about counting slaves for representation?
7. What was the Three-Fifths Compromise?
8. What states opposed ending the African slave trade?
9. What compromise was reached on the African slave trade?
10. What agreement was reached about slaves who escaped across state lines?

NATIONAL STANDARDS CORRELATIONS:

<u>NCSS VIb:</u> (Power, Authority, & Governance) Describe the purpose of government and how its powers are acquired, used, and justified.

<u>NSH Era 3, Standard 3:</u> The institutions and practices of government created during the Revolution and how they were revised between 1787 and 1815 to create the foundation of the American political system based on the U.S. Constitution and the Bill of Rights

WEBSITES:

http://www.yale.edu.lawweb/avalon/states/statutes/pennst01.htm
"An Act for the Gradual Abolition of Slavery (1)," The Avalon Project at Yale Law School

http://www.csusm.edu/Black_Excellence/documentary/pg-s-a-revolution.html
"Chapter 4: All Men Are Created Equal," California State University, San Marcos

http://www.digitalhistory.uh.edu/learning_history/revolution/revolution_slavery.cfm
"Activity 6: Slavery, the American Revolution, and the Constitution," Digital History

Some African-Americans Defy Stereotypes

Gustavus Vassa

Liberals like Jefferson were puzzled about the apparent conflict between their own ideals and the ownership of slaves. In a letter written in 1814, Jefferson wrote Phillis Wheatley that, compared to British workers, slaves "are better fed in these States, warmer clothed, and labor less than the ... day laborers of England." Others liked to quote the Greek philosopher Aristotle, who divided mankind into masters and slaves. Masters were capable of thinking, and when they gave orders to the slave class, it did them no harm, because the slaves were incapable of thinking for themselves. Some argued that taking the slaves from the primitive society of Africa and bringing them to America gave them the benefits of a better life on Earth and in the hereafter. Alexis de Tocqueville, author of *Democracy in America*, observed that since American slavery was based on race, its effect was different than it had been in ancient societies where freedom alone separated free from slave. With race mixed into the issue, "the law may cancel servitude, God alone can obliterate its brand."

When any African-American stepped out from the crowd and showed that he or she could grasp a complex idea and express himself or herself well in writing or speech, that action weakened the premise that Africans were, by nature, inferior. Stereotypes may not be destroyed, but they can be weakened.

Gustavus Vassa (1745–1801) was born in Africa, but he was taken as a slave to Barbados and then to Virginia. Sold to a ship captain, he was then taken to England. His master was angered when Vassa asked about buying his freedom, and he sold Vassa in the West Indies to a Quaker merchant. His new master trained him in math, so he could become a clerk. After purchasing his freedom, Vassa went to England and became a ship captain. He later managed a Jamaican plantation and was in charge of a British expedition to return African-Americans to Africa. He was an excellent writer, touching the conscience of Queen Charlotte with an appeal on behalf of West Indian slaves.

Phillis Wheatley (c.1753–1784), also born in Africa, was sold as a slave in Boston when she was eight years old. She soon impressed her master with her intelligence. Without the benefit of formal education, she was able to read the Bible within 16 months of her arrival. Then she began to read Greek and Roman history, translating Ovid from Latin. It was in poetry that she excelled, and her talent was celebrated in New England and England. Even General Washington wrote her a letter praising her poetry.

Benjamin Banneker (1731–1806) was born free in Maryland and used the little formal education he received to great advantage. He was a biologist, astronomer, and engineer. His most important achievement was working with Pierre L'Enfant in laying out the streets of Washington, D.C.

RESULTS: Isolated examples did not influence many white attitudes about African-Americans, but their achievements did inspire other African-Americans to excel in the future.

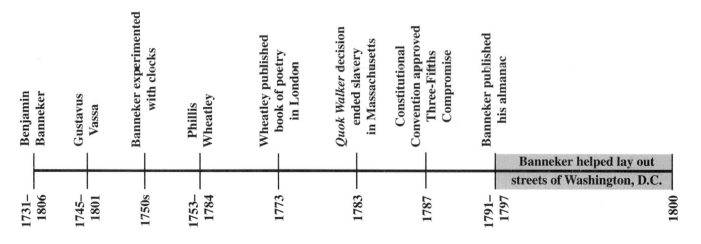

1731–1806	1745–1801	1750s	1753–1784	1773	1783	1787	1791–1797	1800
Benjamin Banneker	Gustavus Vassa	Banneker experimented with clocks	Phillis Wheatley	Wheatley published book of poetry in London	*Quok Walker* decision ended slavery in Massachusetts	Constitutional Convention approved Three-Fifths Compromise	Banneker published his almanac	Banneker helped lay out streets of Washington, D.C.

Name: _____   Date: _____

Some African-Americans Defy Stereotypes: Reinforcement

Directions: Complete the following activities, essays, and challenges on your own paper.

ACTIVITIES:

1. Discuss stereotypes, and have the class give examples.
2. Begin a list of African-Americans who managed to accomplish major things in different fields.

ESSAYS:

1. What stereotypes about African-American intelligence did Vassa, Wheatley, and Banneker challenge?
2. Why are stereotypes important, and why is showing that the stereotype is wrong important to those with a poor image?
3. Why did Alexis de Tocqueville believe it would be harder to erase the effects of slavery in the United States than in the ancient world? Do you agree with him?

CHALLENGES:

1. How did Jefferson justify owning slaves?
2. Why did Aristotle think some people were meant to be slaves?
3. Why did Alexis de Tocqueville feel American slavery was different from ancient slavery?
4. How did Vassa make his ship captain master angry with him; what happened because of it?
5. What job did Vassa have in Jamaica?
6. How did Phillis Wheatley convince her master that she had remarkable ability?
7. In what type of literature did Phillis Wheatley excel as a writer?
8. Who gave special praise to Miss Wheatley?
9. What scientific fields did Benjamin Banneker study?
10. With whom did Benjamin Banneker work, and what did he accomplish on his most important work?

NATIONAL STANDARDS CORRELATIONS:

NCSS IVg: (Individual Development & Identity) Identify and interpret examples of stereotyping, conformity, and altruism.
NSH Era 2, Standard 3: How the values and institutions of European economic life took root in the colonies, and how slavery reshaped European and African life in the Americas

WEBSITES:

http://memory.loc.gov/ammem/aaohtml/exhibit/aopart2.html
"Free Blacks in the Antebellum Period," The Library of Congress

http://darkwing.uoregon.edu/~rbear/wheatley.html
"Poems: Phillis Wheatley," The University of Oregon

http://memory.loc.gov/ammem/today/nov09.html
"Today in History: November 9," The Library of Congress

The Cotton Gin and Slavery

After the adoption of the Constitution, it appeared that the need for slaves was in decline. Nevertheless, when slaves escaped, their masters wanted them back. Congress passed the Fugitive Slave Act of 1793 to make the process easier. The law allowed the owner to capture runaways, take them before a federal or state magistrate, and obtain a certificate allowing the master to take them back to their home state. There was no trial by jury, and slaves could not testify.

Eli Whitney's original cotton gin

Whether slavery itself would continue depended not on federal policy but on economic need. Tobacco, the main crop demanding slave labor, was depleting the soil, so less slaves were needed. Rice production was limited to the South Carolina and Georgia coastline. The only other crop requiring extensive slave labor was cotton. There were two types of cotton: upland and sea island. The latter was the best quality and the easiest to clean (remove seeds), but it had only a limited area where it could be grown on the mainland. Upland cotton could be grown in a wider area, but its seeds were difficult to remove from the boll.

In 1792, a Yale graduate named Eli Whitney was hired as a tutor by a Georgia planter; but when he arrived, he found the position had already been filled. He was then invited to travel with Mrs. Nathaniel Greene, the widow of a Revolutionary War general, to her estate. While there, he earned his keep by repairing plantation equipment. He was told one evening about the problem of removing seeds, and he went to work inventing a cotton engine (gin for short). In April 1793, it was ready for use. It was a simple box with a hand crank, but it would do the work in hours that had taken days before. Now upland cotton could be profitably grown. Soon there were thousands of gins built by either Whitney or his competitors.

The timing was important. Samuel Slater had recently (1790) set up a cotton mill in Rhode Island. To thrive, his mill demanded a larger supply of cotton than that being produced. Now, with Whitney's cotton gin and the many imitators that were soon on the market, cotton production soared. Cotton did not require heavy machinery, so a small farmer could grow it as well as a big farmer. However, it was a crop that wore out soil, so those with enough money to buy the land bought more than they needed.

In England and the North, textile mills had a great appetite for the South's cotton, and it seemed like a business that always thrived. Cotton plantations began to spread from the coast of Georgia to Mississippi. These were businesses, and the communities they created were "company towns." On many plantations, the master was seldom around, and the overseers were in charge.

RESULTS: Cotton became "king" in the South, and over half of the slaves were involved in its production. The plantation system was much more common than it would have been otherwise, and slavery became a big business.

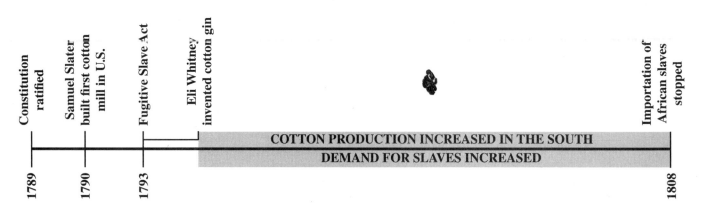

Name: _____   Date: _____

The Cotton Gin and Slavery: Reinforcement

Directions: Complete the following activities, essays, and challenges on your own paper.

ACTIVITIES:

1. Discuss how technology can have social consequences. You might use the automobile or a clock as examples.
2. Show the students a map of where cotton is grown. Have a student research cotton and report the findings to the class.

ESSAYS:

1. Give an example of a modern machine that has changed the way people live. Tell how it has affected society.
2. Do you think inventors have a responsibility to see that their machines do not have a harmful impact on society? Why?
3. As a slave, would you have been glad or unhappy when your master bought a cotton gin? Why?

CHALLENGES:

1. Was it hard or easy for a master to claim a slave under the Fugitive Slave Act of 1793?
2. Before cotton replaced it, what was the southern crop requiring the most slave labor?
3. Why was southern rice production so low?
4. What were the two major varieties of cotton?
5. Where did the name "gin" come from?
6. Who built the first cotton mill in the United States?
7. What did the Fugitive Slave Act and the cotton gin have in common?
8. How large an area was involved in large-scale cotton production?
9. What were the main markets for cotton?
10. How many slaves were involved in producing cotton?

NATIONAL STANDARDS CORRELATIONS:

NCSS VIIIb: (Science, Technology, & Society) Show through specific examples how science and technology have changed people's perceptions of the social and natural world, such as in their relationship to land, animal life, family life, and economic needs, wants, and security.

NSH Era 4, Standard 2: How the industrial revolution, increasing immigration, the rapid expansion of slavery, and the westward movement changed the lives of Americans and led toward regional tensions

WEBSITES:

http://www.cr.nps.gov/delta/underground/slave.htm
"African-Americans in Slavery," National Park Service

http://www.eliwhitney.org/cotton.htm
"The Cotton Gin," The Eli Whitney Museum

http://www.ku.edu/carrie/docs/texts/fugslave.htm
"Fugitive Slave Law of 1793," The University of Kansas

Slaves Find Power in Religion

Karl Marx called religion "the opiate of the masses," and some slave-owners tried to use it that way—to make slaves docile and more concerned about the heaven to come than about their suffering on Earth. Other masters introduced their slaves to Christianity as part of their obligation to bring the world to Christ. There were still other owners who saw potential harm in slave religion and did not want their slaves in church or at evangelistic meetings. In religion, slaves found the hope and power denied them everywhere else. There was a God above their master—one who would someday even the score for the suffering the slave had endured.

Religious revival

Southern churches often had slave members. Seated in the balcony, or in the back if there was no balcony, slaves sometimes attended services with their masters. On plantations, the master might bring a white minister to preach a special message to the slaves. The usual topics would be the need to obey, not to steal chickens, proper morality, or church doctrine. As emotional religious revivals, like the one at Cane Ridge, Kentucky, swept the South, masters and slaves attended and "got religion" together.

White ministers might speak to the slaves, but it was the slave preachers who commanded the attention of the congregation. They were slaves, too, and under the watchful eye of the master. If they spoke too boldly in worship services in the slave quarter, they were subject to a flogging, so care was taken not to offend the master or overseer who stood at the door. However, informal services away from scrutiny took place around campfires in the woods at night.

Hymns that pleased whites did not always appeal to the African-Americans, so they developed their own. They became totally involved in the beat, clapping hands, keeping time with their feet, and tossing their heads. Slaves created new words to songs as they went along. In the singing and chanting, they experienced a freedom that slavery denied them.

The most common song of the slave was the *spiritual*. Most of these songs expressed a hidden meaning that was clear enough to slaves but was hidden from white observers. "Go down, Moses ... tell ole pharaoh, let my people go," could easily have substituted "master" for "pharaoh." Slaves being sold away from family and friends sang, "When we all meet in heaven, there is no parting there." In "O Canaan, sweet Canaan, I am bound for the land of Canaan," it was perhaps the North, not Canaan, that they were thinking about. The "day of jubilee," so often sung about in spirituals, was about the day slavery ended and not when life ended.

RESULTS: Facing lives of endless toil and with no assurance that anything would ever improve in their lives, slaves found in religion the promise that God cared and would give them their just reward at the end of life. In the meantime, Jesus was by their side suffering with them.

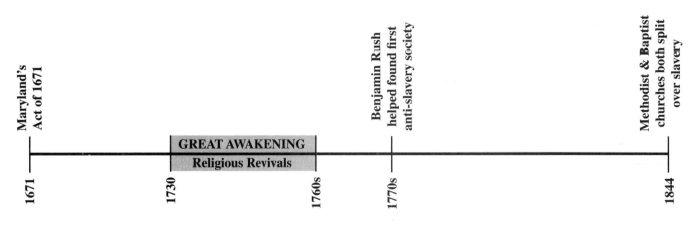

Maryland's Act of 1671

GREAT AWAKENING
Religious Revivals

Benjamin Rush helped found first anti-slavery society

Methodist & Baptist churches both split over slavery

1671 — 1730 — 1760s — 1770s — 1844

Name: _____ Date: _____

Slaves Find Power in Religion: Reinforcement

Directions: Complete the following activities, essays, and challenges on your own paper.

ACTIVITIES:

1. Listen to some spirituals, and see if you can detect any hidden meaning.
2. Listen to a speech or sermon by Jesse Jackson, Martin Luther King, Jr., or some other eloquent African-American minister, and notice the rhythm and colorful imagery used.

ESSAYS:

1. Why did some slaveowners have reason to fear their slaves becoming religious?
2. What arguments could you give that religion actually made slaves more rebellious?
3. What arguments could you give that religion helped masters control their slaves?

CHALLENGES:

1. What did slaves find in religion that they could not find elsewhere?
2. Where did slaves sit when they attended a white church service?
3. What would be the type of topic when a white minister preached to slaves?
4. Why were slave preachers careful when they conducted a worship service in the slave quarters?
5. What made slave religious music different from white hymns?
6. What was the most common type of slave music?
7. In the spiritual "Go Down, Moses," what term could have been used for pharaoh?
8. When they sang about "Canaan," what could have they really been singing about?
9. What day were they singing about in the "day of jubilee"?
10. When did slaves believe they would get their just reward?

NATIONAL STANDARDS CORRELATIONS:

NCSS Ia: (Culture) Compare similarities and differences in the ways groups, societies, and cultures meet human needs and concerns.
NSH Era 2, Standard 2: How political, religious, and social institutions emerged in the English colonies

WEBSITES:

http://memory.loc.gov/ammem/award99/ncuhtml/csbchome.html
"The Church in the Southern Black Community, 1780–1925," The Library of Congress

http://www.stanford.edu/group/King/index.htm
"The Martin Luther King, Jr., Papers Project," Stanford University

http://xroads.virginia.edu/~HYPER/TWH/Higg.html
"Negro Spirituals," University of Virginia

http://www.pbs.org/wgbh/aia/part2/2narr2.html
"Religion and Slavery," Public Broadcasting Service

Northern African-Americans Form Separate Churches

Richard Allen

Like southern African-Americans, those in the North developed an interest in religion, but unlike the slave, they were free to make choices. Many whites wished the slaves would attend someone else's church, but Christian doctrine makes it hard to justify barring anyone from worshipping. Those churches wishing to discourage African-Americans found ways of making them feel unwelcome. At that time, families owned the pew they used. Some churches required that the pew could only be sold to a "respectable white." The balcony, the "African corner," or the back pews were the only places African-Americans were allowed to sit in most churches.

Richard Allen, a former Delaware slave, traveled with a Methodist evangelist and was then given preaching assignments by Bishop Francis Asbury. His friend, Absalom Jones, a former slave who had purchased his own and his wife's freedom, was with Allen in a Philadelphia church in 1787 when they were insultingly ordered to leave. The two men brought other religious Philadelphian African-Americans together in forming the Free African Society—a mutual benefit organization to help widows and orphans, provide a burial plot for the dead, and support the Pennsylvania Abolition Society. They asked for white support, but that was cut short by criticism from the white churches they had left. They built a church building but could not decide which denomination to join.

Jones and Allen disagreed over which church to join. Jones became the minister of St. Thomas Protestant Episcopal Church—the first African-American congregation in the United States. Allen remained a Methodist, but he and other African-Americans wanted more control over their affairs than the Methodists usually allowed. In 1816, other African-American Methodists met at Allen's Bethel Church and formed the African Methodist Episcopal Church with Allen as its bishop.

Once the process of separating began, some African-American Baptists and Congregationalists in the North began establishing their own churches. Other African-Americans continued attending white churches. Of all denominations, the Roman Catholics were the most consistent in treating African-Americans with respect. Some Quakers, with their tradition of supporting African-Americans, greeted them as equals at their services, but at other Quaker meeting houses, community pressure and perhaps personal bias caused them to either deny membership to African-Americans or to put them in segregated seating.

When an African-American man, Isiah DeGrasse, attended the Protestant Episcopal's General Theological Seminary, the bishop asked him to withdraw. Yet at the Presbyterian Union Theological Seminary, there seemed to be no barriers to African-Americans wishing to attend.

RESULTS: Not all African-Americans liked the idea of separating from white churches. Frederick Douglass in his newspaper *North Star* called them "negro pews, on a higher and larger scale." It would be an issue often argued at a later time, but few can question the importance of African-American churches today.

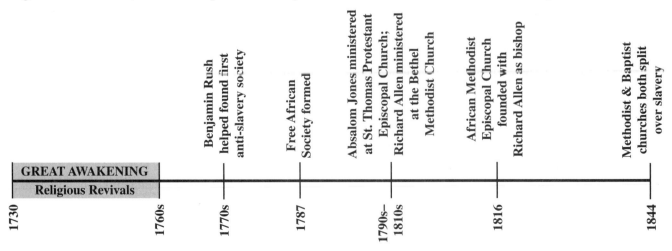

Timeline:

GREAT AWAKENING / **Religious Revivals**

- 1730
- 1760s — Benjamin Rush helped found first anti-slavery society
- 1770s
- 1787 — Free African Society formed
- 1790s–1810s — Absalom Jones ministered at St. Thomas Protestant Episcopal Church; Richard Allen ministered at the Bethel Methodist Church
- 1816 — African Methodist Episcopal Church founded with Richard Allen as bishop
- 1844 — Methodist & Baptist churches both split over slavery

Northern African-Americans Form Separate Churches: Reinforcement

Directions: Complete the following activities, essays, and challenges on your own paper.

ACTIVITIES:

1. Have a debate (discussion) on the decision to form separate African-American churches.
2. Ask the class to discuss problems faced by Northern African-Americans that would require group assistance.

ESSAYS:

1. Why do you think some African-Americans attended white churches even though they were not treated well?
2. As a free African-American in Philadelphia, would you have supported or opposed the creation of the Free African Society? Why?
3. Do you think African-Americans were wise in creating their own congregations? Why?

CHALLENGES:

1. What areas of white churches were often reserved for African-Americans?
2. What training did Richard Allen have before he became a minister?
3. What were the activities of the Free African Society?
4. To which church did Absalom Jones minister, and what was important about that church?
5. At the time that Allen and Jones went their separate ways, which denomination did Allen support?
6. What new branch of the Methodist Church did Allen help form; what was his role in the new church?
7. Which denomination did not segregate at all?
8. When African-Americans attended Quaker meetings, how were they treated?
9. What happened when Isiah DeGrasse attended the General Theological Seminary?
10. How did the Presbyterians' Union Theological Seminary treat African-Americans?

NATIONAL STANDARDS CORRELATIONS:

<u>NCSS IVc:</u> (Individual Development & Identity) Describe the ways family, gender, ethnicity, nationality, and institutional affiliations contribute to personal identity.
<u>NSH Era 2, Standard 2:</u> How political, religious, and social institutions emerged in the English colonies

WEBSITES:

http://www.nhc.rtp.nc.us/tserve/nineteen/nkeyinfo/nafrican.htm
"African-American Religion in the Nineteenth Century," National Humanities Center

http://www.auburn.edu/~lakwean/hist2010/doc1787_freafrsoc.html
"Absalom Jones and Richard Allen, Preamble of the Free African Society, 12 April 1787," Auburn University

http://www.pbs.org/wgbh/aia/part3/3narr3.html
"The Black Church," Public Broadcasting Service

http://earlyamerica.com/review/spring97/allen.html
"Richard Allen and African-American Identity," Archiving Early America

African-Americans Oppose Colonization

No matter what Northern African-Americans did, it seemed that they never received the respect they deserved. During the War of 1812 after the British attacked and burned Washington, Philadelphia leaders, fearing their city was next, turned to African-American leaders for help. James Forten, Bishop Richard Allen, and Absalom Jones recruited over 2,000 African-Americans to build defenses. African-American sailors in Oliver Perry's fleet at the Battle of Lake Erie won his praise. In the South, General Jackson's army at New Orleans included slaves, and they played a key role in blocking the British advance.

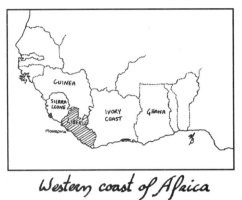

Western coast of Africa

When the peace treaty was signed at Ghent, Belgium, it called for a *status quo ante bellum* (everything remaining as it was at the beginning of the war). Southerners wanted slaves who had escaped to the British returned to their owners or to be paid for the loss if they were not. As for slaves, their lives were the same after the war as they had been before the war. The *status quo* never seemed to change when it pertained to slaves or free African-Americans, North or South.

Paul Cuffe, a wealthy African-American shipowner, became so concerned about the conditions faced by poor African-Americans in Massachusetts that he spent $4,000 of his own money to transport 38 African-Americans back to Africa in 1815.

Many whites were thinking the same way. In 1816, the American Colonization Society (ACS) was formed. Its purpose was to return "free people of color" to Africa. The idea had been around since the early 18th century, and Thomas Jefferson was among those who had long supported it. Among the founders of the ACS were many notable Americans, including Francis Scott Key, Henry Clay, and John Randolph. At the organizational meeting, Elias Caldwell said, "The more you endeavor to improve the condition of these people [free African-Americans], the more you cultivate their minds (unless by religious instruction), the more miserable you make them ..." Many whites, including Quakers and antislavery men, supported the ACS at first.

Endorsed by many national leaders, the ACS raised money to win public support for the project and to buy ships to transport the African-Americans to Africa. In 1820, 88 settlers were sent to an island off the coast of Africa, but many died of malaria before they moved to the mainland. In 1824, the colony was named Liberia, and its capital was Monrovia (named after President James Monroe, an ACS member).

No one asked free African-Americans what they thought about colonizing Africa, but they expressed themselves anyway. About 3,000 free African-Americans gathered in Philadelphia to answer the ACS. In that meeting and others that followed, they replied that they were Americans, and this was their country. "Here we were born, and here we will die." They charged that the only reason for removing free African-Americans to Africa was to keep other African-Americans in slavery.

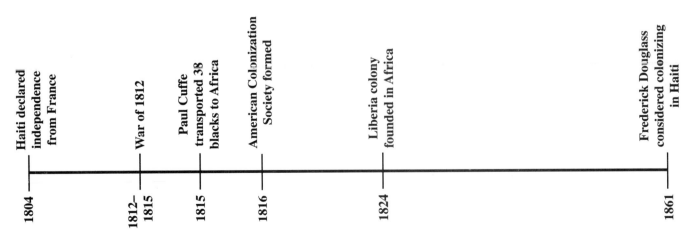

Haiti declared independence from France — 1804

War of 1812 — 1812–1815

Paul Cuffe transported 38 blacks to Africa — 1815

American Colonization Society formed — 1816

Liberia colony founded in Africa — 1824

Frederick Douglass considered colonizing in Haiti — 1861

Name: _____ Date: _____

African-Americans Oppose Colonization: Reinforcement

RESULTS: Shaken by African-American opposition to colonization, African-Americans and antislavery people turned against it. Colonizing, however, remained popular up to the time of the Civil War and many, including Abraham Lincoln, toyed with the idea.

Directions: Complete the following activities, essays, and challenges on your own paper.

ACTIVITIES:

1. Research Liberia and list problems African-Americans would have if they were to colonize there today.
2. Ask the class how they would feel if any group decided *they* should go back to the land of their ancestors.

ESSAYS:

1. As a free African-American born in America, what attitude do you think you would have taken toward colonization?
2. As a white anti-slavery person, why might you have supported the American Colonization Society at first? After African-American protests, would you have changed your mind?
3. As an African-American colonist, what problems do you think you would encounter in going to Africa in 1820?

CHALLENGES:

1. Who organized African-Americans to build defenses for Philadelphia during the War of 1812?
2. Who used slaves in the War of 1812, and in what battle?
3. Why did Paul Cuffe spend $4,000 in 1815?
4. What was the purpose of the American Colonization Society?
5. Who were important early members of the ACS?
6. When did the ACS send the first African-Americans back to Africa? What happened to them?
7. What nation developed because of the ACS?
8. What is the capital of that nation, and how did it get its name?
9. What attitude did the African-Americans who gathered at Philadelphia have about going back to Africa?
10. What motives did African-Americans feel the ACS had behind its program of returning African-Americans to Africa?

NATIONAL STANDARDS CORRELATIONS:

<u>NCSS Vb:</u> (Individuals, Groups, & Institutions) Analyze group and institutional influences on people, events, and elements of culture.

<u>NSH Era 4, Standard 4:</u> The sources and character of cultural, religious, and social reform movements in the antebellum period

WEBSITES:

http://www.loc.gov/exhibits/african/afam002.html
"Colonization," The Library of Congress

http://rs6.log.gov/ammem/gmdhtml/libhtml/liberia.html
"History of Liberia: A Time Line," The Library of Congress

http://memory.loc.gov/ammem/gmdhtml/libhtml/libhome.html
"Maps of Liberia: 1830–1870," The Library of Congress

The Missouri Compromise

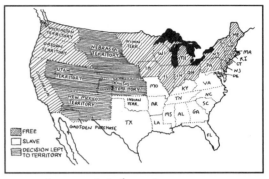

Territories affected by Missouri Compromise

The "Era of Good Feelings" was what they called it—the time when the Federalists were no longer a major factor in elections and before the Republicans divided between the John Q. Adams and Jackson factions. The victory at New Orleans had made up for earlier failures in the War of 1812, and national spirit was running high. President James Monroe won the election of 1816 by a 183–34 margin in electoral votes, and in 1820, the Federalists were so weak they could not even carry a single state in New England.

But if the nation was unified, it was only on the surface. Northern and southern Republicans disagreed on issues like the tariff, federal funding of roads and canals (so-called "internal improvements"), and slavery. Many national leaders wanted to succeed Monroe and were trying to get a political edge. Federalists were hoping that if the right issue came along, the Republicans would split, and the Federalists could regain power.

In 1819, a bill to make Missouri a state came before Congress. The French and Spanish had brought slaves into Missouri before it became part of the Louisiana Purchase in 1803. Other slave states had been admitted recently (Mississippi in 1817, Alabama in 1819) with little debate, but suddenly slavery became a major issue. Arguments began when Representative James Tallmadge of New York offered an amendment to the Missouri Bill that would prohibit new slaves from entering Missouri, and children born of slaves after Missouri's admission would be freed at the age of 25. Tallmadge was Republican, but most supporters of his amendment were Federalists. The Senate, after much debate, removed Tallmadge's limit.

The votes on Tallmadge's proposal were strictly sectional; all votes in favor were cast by northerners, all opposed were by southerners. Jefferson feared the vote was "like a fire bell in the night"—awakening him and filling him with terror.

Senator Jesse Thomas of Illinois proposed a solution that became known as the *Missouri Compromise*. Missouri would enter the Union as a slave state; Maine as a free state. Territory in the Louisiana Purchase south of 36° 30′ (the southern boundary of Missouri) would be open to slavery, and territories north of the line would be closed to slavery.

The ink was hardly dry on the agreement when a new issue came up. Missouri wanted to keep free African-Americans from entering the state. This seemed to go against the Constitution's guarantee that "Citizens of each State shall be entitled to all the Privileges and Immunities of Citizens in the several States." Henry Clay worked out a compromise prohibiting Missouri from barring citizens of other states, but he did not define whether a free African-American was a citizen.

RESULTS: Southerners felt that abolitionists were enlisting other northerners to destroy slavery. They felt they must defend slavery as a state's right under the Constitution.

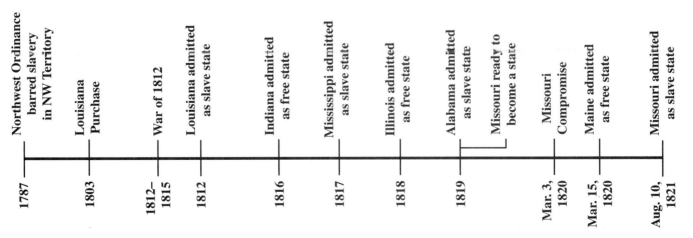

Name: _____ Date: _____

The Missouri Compromise: Reinforcement

Directions: Complete the following activities, essays, and challenges on your own paper.

ACTIVITIES:

1. Examine a map and ask which states could be carved out of the territory south of 36° 30′.
2. Stage a discussion between a northern and southern member of Congress at the time of the Missouri Compromise debate.

ESSAYS:

1. As a member of Congress from the South, why would you have opposed the Tallmadge Amendment to the Missouri Bill?
2. As an abolitionist, why would you have supported the Tallmadge Amendment?
3. Which side (North or South) made the better deal in agreeing to the Missouri Compromise?

CHALLENGES:

1. Who was president during the "Era of Good Feelings"?
2. What were some issues splitting Republicans?
3. What other nations had brought slaves into Missouri before the Louisiana Purchase?
4. Who proposed that no more slaves be brought into Missouri?
5. What party most actively supported the Tallmadge Amendment?
6. Who removed the Tallmadge Amendment from the Missouri Bill?
7. What territories in the Louisiana Purchase were opened to slavery by the Missouri Compromise?
8. What other state entered the Union because of the Missouri Compromise?
9. What group did Missouri want to keep from entering the state?
10. What compromise did Clay work out that made it possible to admit Missouri as a state?

NATIONAL STANDARDS CORRELATIONS:

NCSS VIc: (Power, Authority, & Governance) Analyze and explain ideas and governmental mechanisms to meet needs and wants of citizens, regulate territory, manage conflict, and establish order and security.
NSH Era 4, Standard 3: The extension, restriction, and reorganization of political democracy after 1800

WEBSITES:

http://www.loc.gov/rr/program/bib/ourdocs/Missouri.html
"Missouri Compromise," The Library of Congress

http://www.ourdocuments.gov/doc.php?flash=true&doc=22
"Missouri Compromise (1820)," The U.S. National Archives and Records Administration

http://www.digitalhistory.uh.edu/database/article_display.cfm?HHID=574
"The Era of Good Feelings: The Growth of Political Factionalism and Sectionalism," Digital History

Slaves Make a Life for Themselves

The picture of slavery is one blurred by the passing of time; all of the masters and slaves are gone. No effort was made to record the words of slaves until the 1930s when most had died, and those old enough to remember were in their 80s and 90s. Few slaves wrote about their experiences; eloquent writers like Frederick Douglass and William Wells Brown were the exceptions.

To understand life in slavery, the modern person has to remember that both master and slave were humans and, like anyone else, personalities varied. Some masters tried to treat slaves well. George Washington freed his slaves in his will; Thomas Jefferson's slaves lived in brick cottages; Jefferson Davis's slaves governed themselves with slave-run trial courts.

The Fiddler

Harsh slaveowners also existed. They half-starved their slaves, worked them hard, whipped them often, treated them worse than cattle, and enjoyed making life miserable. When a master was cruel, his slaves had no legal protection from his brutal treatment.

Plantation slaves often had little contact with their masters. Their supervisors were drivers and overseers. *Drivers* were slaves who were made into bosses by their master, so they were in a bad situation. Go easy on the workers, and if the work was not done, the driver would be flogged; if he was too hard on the workers, the driver made enemies among his fellow slaves. *Overseers* were whites who took orders from the master. A few were good managers, but most were not.

Even in the best of circumstances, slaves were property and could be bought, sold, lent, or rented out. Their opportunities to learn and achieve were very limited. They had little personal incentive to work hard; slavery offered little room for promotions.

How did slaves survive the uncertainty and the danger of harsh treatment? They made the best of a bad situation. When masters allowed them to grow gardens, they sold surplus food to whites. During holidays, they worked for pay. They found pleasure in family and friends in the evening.

Music was a relief for them. Slaves made musical instruments from whatever was available. They liked to dance, sing, and play the banjo, drums, or fiddle. When he was interested in a girl, a young man tried to impress her by bringing presents and winning her mother's approval. Sometimes, a dignified marriage performed by a minister would follow; other times, they jumped over a broomstick together. Although the odds were against them, many slaves took their role as husband, wife, or parent seriously.

RESULTS: What slaves could and could not do was limited by the type of master they had. When the master understood that happy workers were more productive, slaves lived better; if the master felt harsh discipline was the only way to treat them, their lives were miserable. Regardless, slaves found ways to adjust to their situations.

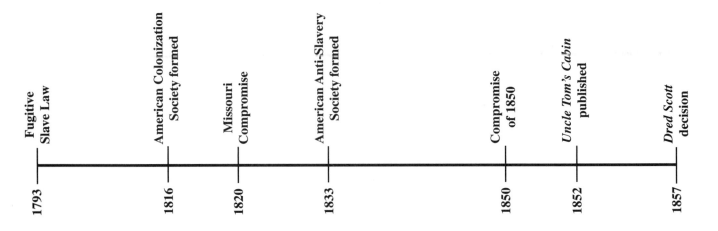

Fugitive Slave Law — 1793
American Colonization Society formed — 1816
Missouri Compromise — 1820
American Anti-Slavery Society formed — 1833
Compromise of 1850 — 1850
Uncle Tom's Cabin published — 1852
Dred Scott decision — 1857

Name: _____ Date: _____

Slaves Make a Life for Themselves: Reinforcement

Directions: Complete the following activities, essays, and challenges on your own paper.

ACTIVITIES:

1. Have the class list instructions from a master to an overseer who is going to take over the plantation in his absence.
2. Have the class pretend that they are slaves. Discuss the advice they would give their younger brothers and sisters.

ESSAYS:

1. Even though some slaveowners tried to be kind, why was slavery never a kindly way for one human to treat another?
2. Why do you think some owners were so cruel to their slaves?
3. Why would being a driver be a difficult position?

CHALLENGES:

1. Why were the interviews conducted with former slaves in the 1930s not as accurate as they might have been?
2. Name two former slaves who wrote about their experiences.
3. What owner supplied brick cottages for his slaves?
4. What were African-American supervisors called?
5. What were white supervisors called?
6. In what ways were slaves property?
7. What were some ways slaves earned money?
8. What were popular musical instruments among the slaves?
9. When a male slave liked a girl, how did he try to attract her?
10. What was the simplest form of the marriage ceremony?

NATIONAL STANDARDS CORRELATIONS:

NCSS IIe: (Time, Continuity, & Change) Develop critical sensitivities such as empathy and skepticism regarding attitudes, values, and behaviors of people in different historical contexts.
NSH Era 4, Standard 2: How the industrial revolution, increasing immigration, the rapid expansion of slavery, and the westward movement changed the lives of Americans and led toward regional tensions

WEBSITES:

http://memory.loc.gov/learn/features/civilrights/learn_more.html
"From Slavery to Civil Rights: A Timeline of African-American History," Library of Congress

http://www.sciway.net/hist/chicora/slavery18-1.html
"Understanding Slavery: The Lives of Eighteenth Century African-Americans," Chicora Foundation

http://www.pbs.org/wnet/slavery/experience/living/index.html
"The Slave Experience: Living Conditions," Public Broadcasting Service

Slaves Rebel in Different Ways

While some people will always put up with a cruel system, others will not. As masters were not all good or bad, slaves were not all obedient or rebels, either. When slaves did not like their master or overseer, they had ways of getting revenge. One way to do it was by loafing—pretending to be sick might get them out of a day's work. Other ways were by breaking tools so they could not work, stealing from the master, or deliberately leaving a gate open so livestock would get loose. Spreading gossip was another method, and it did not take long for slaves and whites to hear that "Massa' Jones' wife went after him with a skillet when he was drunk."

Slaves loafing

Learning to read and write was another form of rebellion. Whites feared that if slaves became educated, they could forge passes, read abolitionist newspapers, and begin to think for themselves. Some slaves learned to read from white children studying their lessons or from kind mistresses who wanted to teach them how to read the Bible. To most slaves, reading print on a page was what separated the free from the slave, and they wanted to know how to do it.

Violence was also a possible response. One example was Denmark Vesey, a former slave who won enough money in a lottery to buy his freedom. His hatred for slavery and admiration for Toussaint L'Ouverture led him to organize an 1822 slave revolt in Charleston, South Carolina. Keeping the plans in a small circle of advisors, he recruited slaves through cell leaders. Two weeks before the planned date of rebellion, a house slave informed his master of the plot, and its members were rounded up. Vesey refused to give any information to his captors, and he was executed.

Nat Turner was born in 1800, the year of Gabriel Prosser's rebellion. Turner had some education, and he became convinced that he had been chosen to free the slaves from bondage. He saw signs in the heavens and on leaves and planned his attack for August 21, 1831. With seven other slaves, he attacked his master's family and killed them. Then the slaves scattered and, in one day and night, killed approximately 60 whites. A white response developed quickly, and the revolt collapsed; but Turner had disappeared. Rumors spread throughout the South that Turner was "in the neighborhood," and that caused many sleepless nights. Actually, Turner was hidden away about two miles from where the revolt began. Turner and most of the other leaders involved in the plot were eventually caught and executed.

During Turner's trial, it was charged that he had read the abolitionist newspaper *The Liberator,* and fear spread that Nat Turner's rebellion was the result of northern agitators. No evidence exists to support the fear, but the South knew it had others besides slaves to watch from now on.

RESULTS: Slaves developed methods of resistance that evened the score with the system that held them down. The Veseys and Turners were few in number, but their mere existence was enough to cause white concern.

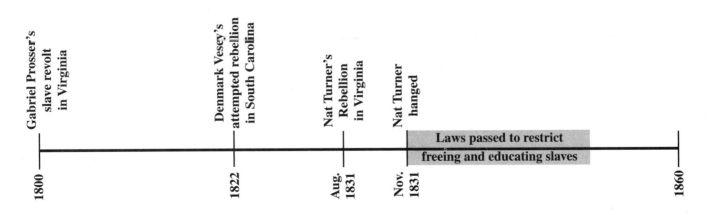

Gabriel Prosser's slave revolt in Virginia — 1800

Denmark Vesey's attempted rebellion in South Carolina — 1822

Nat Turner's Rebellion in Virginia — Aug. 1831

Nat Turner hanged — Nov. 1831

Laws passed to restrict freeing and educating slaves

1860

Name: _____ Date: _____

Slaves Rebel in Different Ways: Reinforcement

Directions: Complete the following activities, essays, and challenges on your own paper.

ACTIVITIES:

1. Ask the students how *they* rebel when they don't want to do something and they don't want to be punished.
2. Have the students make a list of problems slaves would have in organizing a large-scale slave revolt.

ESSAYS:

1. Discuss ways in which slaves were most likely to rebel without getting punished.
2. As a white southerner of that time, how would you explain the Vesey and Nat Turner rebellions to a northern relative?
3. You are a slave, and someone tells you there is going to be a rebellion. What thoughts go through your head as you decide whether or not to join with the others?

CHALLENGES:

1. What were some quiet ways for slaves to rebel?
2. Why were whites so concerned about slaves learning to read and write?
3. How did Vesey become free?
4. Where did the Vesey revolt take place?
5. How did Nat Turner know "the time was right"?
6. How many whites were killed in Nat Turner's rebellion?
7. After slaves involved in Nat Turner's rebellion were rounded up, why were whites still scared?
8. What happened to the leaders of Nat Turner's rebellion?
9. What newspaper had Turner supposedly read?
10. Who, besides slaves, did the South fear after Nat Turner's rebellion?

NATIONAL STANDARDS CORRELATIONS:

<u>NCSS Id:</u> (Culture) Explain why individuals and groups respond differently to their physical and social environments and/or changes to them on the basis of shared assumptions, values, and beliefs.
<u>NSH Era 4, Standard 2:</u> How the industrial revolution, increasing immigration, the rapid expansion of slavery, and the westward movement changed the lives of Americans and led toward regional tensions

WEBSITES:

http://historymatters.gmu.edu/d/6811/
"The Nat Turner Rebellion," George Mason University

http://www.lva.lib.va.us/whoweare/exhibits/DeathLiberty/natturner/
"Nat Turner's Rebellion," The Library of Virginia

http://memory.loc.gov/cig-bin/query/r?ammem/aaodyssey:@field(NUMBER+@band(rbcmisc+ody0108))
The Confessions of Nat Turner, the Leader of the Late Insurrection in Southampton, Virginia," The Library of Congress

The Abolition Movement

Frederick Douglass had been raised as a slave in Maryland. He had both kind and cruel masters, had been taught to read and write, and had worked as a field hand, a house servant, and a caulker in a Baltimore shipyard. In 1838, he escaped to New York City, then to New Bedford, Connecticut. There he began reading William Lloyd Garrison's *The Liberator*. Douglass had heard of "abolitionists" when he was a slave but had never met one until now. In 1841, he went to the meeting of the Massachusetts Anti-Slavery Society at Nantucket, and he was asked to speak. Despite his nervousness, he spoke, and a crowd of white people listened. He had found new friends, and he went on to become a leader in the movement.

Frederick Douglass

Anti-slavery people had been around for years, and their supporters included many southerners. For people like Benjamin Rush and Thomas Jefferson, slavery was like a knot that could not be untied. Abolitionists would not bother to untie it; they would take an ax to it. Different names have been suggested as the founders of the movement. Some argue it began with the African-Americans protesting colonization. Others believe it began with David Walker, who published *Walker's Appeal* in 1829, urging a violent end to slavery. Still others say it began when Charles Grandison Finney brought his western revival to New York in 1830. His attacks on slavery brought Arthur and Lewis Tappan, wealthy merchants, to the anti-slavery cause.

Whoever began it, William Lloyd Garrison became its lightning rod. He was a strange man in many ways, but he was fearless in the abolition cause. The first edition of *The Liberator* came out in 1831, and it continued until slavery ended in 1865. Garrison helped Douglass get started as a speaker and writer. Douglass soon became so effective that he went out on his own, and he published his autobiography and edited his own newspaper, *The North Star*. For many years, he was the spokesman for African-Americans.

William Wells Brown, son of a slave woman, worked for the abolitionist editor Elijah Lovejoy. Brown went on to become an able speaker for the American Anti-Slavery Society, as well as a journalist and historian.

Women also joined the abolition cause. Two white sisters, Sarah and Angelina Grimke, were daughters of a South Carolina slaveowner, and they discovered that they had an African-American brother. They moved to the North and became outspoken critics of slavery. Harriet Tubman and Sojourner Truth, both of whom were former slaves, were also very active abolitionists.

Politically, the movement did not have much influence in Congress until it found two able spokesmen: Joshua Giddings and John Q. Adams. The former president had so much prestige that he was known as "Old Man Eloquent." When he spoke against slavery, others listened.

RESULTS: Abolitionists had many enemies in both the North and South. These enemies often considered them cranks trying to stir up trouble, and they were right! Like many reformers, they would not be silenced until victory was theirs.

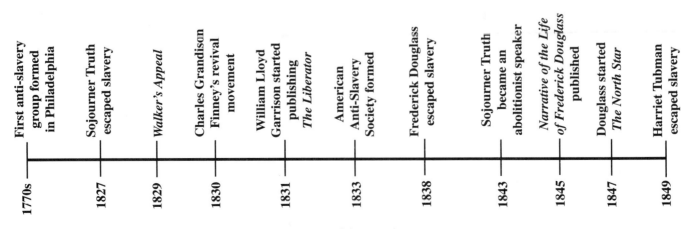

1770s	1827	1829	1830	1831	1833	1838	1843	1845	1847	1849
First anti-slavery group formed in Philadelphia	Sojourner Truth escaped slavery	*Walker's Appeal*	Charles Grandison Finney's revival movement	William Lloyd Garrison started publishing *The Liberator*	American Anti-Slavery Society formed	Frederick Douglass escaped slavery	Sojourner Truth became an abolitionist speaker	*Narrative of the Life of Frederick Douglass* published	Douglass started *The North Star*	Harriet Tubman escaped slavery

Name: _____ Date: _____

The Abolition Movement: Reinforcement

Directions: Complete the following activities, essays, and challenges on your own paper.

ACTIVITIES:

1. Today we have movements that are not popular with many people. Ask if the class would support: a homeless shelter being placed next door, the position of animal rights activists, or those who would protect endangered species at the cost of jobs. This should help them realize how causes create tensions.
2. Research some of the people mentioned in this section.

ESSAYS:

1. Why would an escaped slave like Frederick Douglass have reason to worry about speaking up too much against slavery?
2. David Walker's idea of using violence to end slavery was not approved by most abolitionists. Would you have supported Walker or his critics?
3. Giddings and Adams were both members of the Whig party. Why do you think their support for abolition was not popular with many party members in Congress?

CHALLENGES:

1. What newspaper did Douglass read when he was freed?
2. Where did Douglass give his first speech?
3. Why was Walker unpopular in the South?
4. Who was the "lightning rod" of the abolition movement?
5. What newspaper did Douglass own and edit?
6. With whom did William Wells Brown work?
7. Who was the "sister team" in the movement?
8. Name two African-American women who were abolitionists.
9. Who were two strong voices in the House of Representatives supporting the anti-slavery cause?
10. Who was known as "Old Man Eloquent"?

NATIONAL STANDARDS CORRELATIONS:

NCSS Va: (Individuals, Groups, & Institutions) Demonstrate an understanding of concepts such as role, status, and social class in describing the interactions of individuals and social groups.
NSH Era 4, Standard 4: The sources and character of cultural, religious, and social reform movements in the antebellum period

WEBSITES:

http://memory.loc.gov/ammem/doughtml/doughome.html
"The Frederick Douglass Papers," The Library of Congress

http://www.history.rochester.edu/class/douglass/home.html
"Frederick Douglass: 'Abolitionist/Editor'," University of Rochester

http://www.nps.gov/frdo/fdlife/htm
"The Life of Frederick Douglass," National Park Service

Slavery Debates in Congress

Henry Clay

Abolitionists were agitators trying to stir up a response. In the first issue of *The Liberator,* William Lloyd Garrison wrote: "I will be as harsh as truth and as uncompromising as justice." He never let up. Other abolitionists were also determined, and they paid a price for it. Garrison was put in jail to protect him from a Boston mob. The home of Arthur and Lewis Tappan was burned to the ground. Elijah Lovejoy, editor of the *Alton Observer,* was killed by a mob. The attitude of the federal and local governments was generally hostile to abolitionists, but they still found ways to get their message across. The more enemies tried to silence them, the more ways they found to be heard, and the more friends they made.

Beginning around 1836, government began to notice them. President Jackson approved the postmaster-general's order that abolitionist material could not be delivered in the South unless the addressee requested it. The House of Representatives passed the "gag rule," which prevented any petition regarding slavery from being considered. John Q. Adams, the former president and now a member of the House, led the fight against the gag rule, and it was repealed in 1844.

In 1836, Texas gained independence from Mexico, and many in the South wanted to add Texas to the Union. The North's negative reaction to allowing so large a slaveholding region into the United States caused President Andrew Jackson to back off from the issue. In the 1844 presidential campaign, James K. Polk's platform favored expansion to both Texas and Oregon; when he was elected, Congress approved annexing Texas in 1845. That action caused even more tension between the United States and Mexico; the Mexican War was about to be fought.

When war was declared in 1846, Representative David Wilmot of Pennsylvania proposed that slavery would be prohibited in any territory taken from Mexico. Known as the Wilmot Proviso, it caused bitter debate between North and South before it passed the House; however, it was defeated in the Senate.

The Mexican War ended in 1848, with the United States owning 530,000 square miles of new territory. The California gold rush in 1849 quickly increased its population, and by 1850 the issue of admitting California to the Union was before Congress. The South opposed statehood for California because it would make more free states than slave states in the Senate. Many issues were added to make up the Compromise of 1850, which was worked out by Henry Clay and Stephen Douglas. It was important to slavery because of four provisions: (1) California would be a free state; (2) New Mexico and Utah territories could choose to be slave or free (popular sovereignty); (3) A stronger Fugitive Slave Act was included, and (4) Slave trade was ended in Washington, D.C. The new Fugitive Slave Act required that there be no jury trial, an African-American could not testify in his own defense, and it authorized federal marshals to assemble posses to catch runaways.

RESULTS: The slavery issue, instead of quieting down, was becoming louder, and many Northerners were beginning to listen. Most Northern whites still considered abolitionists radicals, but they were gaining.

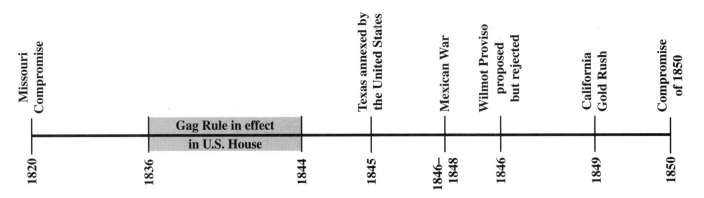

Name: _____ Date: _____

Slavery Debates in Congress: Reinforcement

Directions: Complete the following activities, essays, and challenges on your own paper.

ACTIVITIES:

1. The gag rule backfired on southerners. Have the class discuss how they would have handled abolitionists.
2. Have the class analyze the Compromise of 1850 as free African-Americans living in the North.

ESSAYS:

1. Why would the gag rule anger many people who were not abolitionists?
2. As an abolitionist, why would you oppose annexing Texas?
3. Why would the South react so strongly against the Wilmot Proviso?

CHALLENGES:

1. Who wrote: "I will be as harsh as truth and as uncompromising as justice"?
2. Who was the editor of the *Alton Observer*?
3. What was the purpose of the gag rule?
4. Who led the fight against the gag rule?
5. How long was the time span between Texas independence and its annexation to the United States?
6. What was the purpose of the Wilmot Proviso?
7. Why was the South opposed to making California a state?
8. Who put together the Compromise of 1850?
9. What was "popular sovereignty"?
10. What did the South think they gained from the Compromise of 1850?

NATIONAL STANDARDS CORRELATIONS:

NCSS VIa: (Power, Authority, & Governance) Examine persistent issues involving the rights, roles, and status of the individual in relation to the general welfare.
NSH Era 4, Standard 3: The extension, restriction, and reorganization of political democracy after 1800

WEBSITES:

http://www.archives.gov/exhibits/treasures_of_congress/text/page10_text.html
"Struggles over Slavery: The 'Gag' Rule," The U.S. National Archives and Records Administration

http://www.uschs.org/04_history/subs_articles/04e_09.html
"John Quincy Adams' Congressional Career," The United States Capitol Historical Society

http://lincoln.lib.niu.edu/digitalabolitionism.html
"Abolitionism," Abraham Lincoln Historical Digitization Project

http://www.senate.gov/artandhistory/history/minute/Gag_Rule.htm
"1801–1850: March 16, 1836, Gag Rule," U.S. Senate

The Underground Railroad

Harriet Tubman

The 250,000 free African-Americans of the North lived very uncertain lives. Many, like Frederick Douglass, had escaped from slavery. Others had "freedom papers" showing that they had been emancipated (legally freed). States with personal liberty laws made it difficult for slavecatchers to capture slaves and take them South. But when owners were determined, they stopped at nothing to get their slaves back. Anthony Burns fled from slavery in 1853 and was captured in Boston by a U.S. marshal the next year. Abolitionists in the city protested loudly, and the day he was taken to the ship, Boston went into mourning.

The Burns case was different from most. In the North, many whites had strong feelings against African-Americans. This was especially true of poor immigrants in the cities, who did not like competing against African-Americans for jobs, and true of the "butternuts"—Southern-born farmers living north of the Ohio River. Some made a living out of catching and returning slaves. In the southern states, there were whites who would persuade African-Americans that they were friends, capture them, and then take them to farmers who did not ask questions about the "merchandise" they were buying.

Slaves were suspicious of whites who told them about the "Underground Railroad" that would take them to freedom. The Underground Railroad was composed of volunteers who would hide slaves traveling north to Canada. Slaves were hidden during daylight hours at stops along the route and, using the North Star, they moved in the dark to the next location 10 or 15 miles north. Until they reached Canada, they were never completely safe. If they were caught by a slave catcher or U.S. Marshal, they would be returned to their master, who would probably make a great display of flogging them. It was risky for whites to be involved, but it was even more dangerous for African-Americans who helped slaves to escape. Facing a death sentence if they were captured, it took great courage for them to help slaves escape.

Josiah Henson, a runaway slave, worked as an "agent" on the Railroad, helping over 200 slaves to escape. John Mason, a fugitive from Kentucky, left the safety of Canada to rescue over 1,300 slaves. The most famous of the African-American agents was Harriet Tubman, a clever woman. It is said that she rescued 300 slaves in 19 trips through the South. She would boast, "I nebber run de train off de track, and I nebber lost a passenger." Some passengers lost their nerve and wanted to turn back. She would point a pistol at their heads and say, "You go on or die."

No one knows how many slaves were rescued or how many agents helped them to freedom. One estimate is that 100,000 took the Railroad north to freedom, aided by 3,200 workers. It was rarely helpful to slaves in the Deep South, but it did rescue many from the Upper South.

RESULTS: Slaves escaped, and southerners became obsessed by the Underground Railroad. Not many boarded it, but the South was alarmed by the number of slaves who did manage to escape through it.

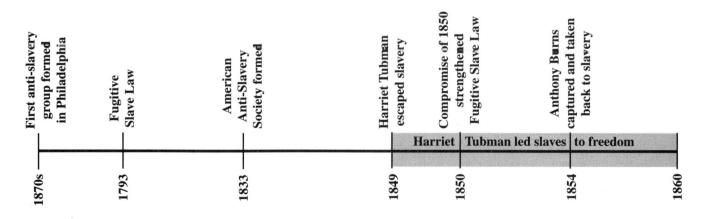

Name: _____ Date: _____

The Underground Railroad: Reinforcement

Directions: Complete the following activities, essays, and challenges on your own paper.

ACTIVITIES:

1. Slaves on the Underground Railroad were moved mostly at night. Blindfold a member of the class, and have some of his or her classmates be guides. Have new guides as the student moves north to freedom.
2. Have the class list dangers that faced a runaway slave heading north over the Railroad.

ESSAYS:

1. As a "stationmaster" on the Underground Railroad, where would you hide slaves so no one would get suspicious?
2. You are a slave, and an Underground Railroad agent tells you he can help you reach freedom. What thoughts would you have about going with him?
3. What threats were there to runaways using the Railroad?

CHALLENGES:

1. Why were freedom papers important to a Northern African-American?
2. What slave was captured in Boston in 1854?
3. Who were "butternuts"?
4. Why were slaves reluctant to go with a white who said he worked for the Underground Railroad?
5. Why was the North Star important to runaways?
6. Why was it dangerous for African-Americans to be involved in the Underground Railroad?
7. What did John Mason do?
8. How many trips did Harriet Tubman make into the South, and how many slaves did she rescue?
9. It is estimated that about how many slaves escaped over the Underground Railroad?
10. It is estimated that about how many agents worked for the Underground Railroad?

NATIONAL STANDARDS CORRELATIONS:

NCSS Ve: (Individuals, Groups, & Institutions) Identify and describe examples of tensions between belief systems and government policies and laws.
NSH Era 4, Standard 2: How the industrial revolution, increasing immigration, the rapid expansion of slavery, and the westward movement changed the lives of Americans and led toward regional tensions

WEBSITES:

http://www.cr.nps.gov/aahistory/ugrr/ugrr.htm
"Our Shared History African-American Heritage: Underground Railroad," National Park Service

http://www.library.cornell.edu/mayantislavery/maysearch.htm
"Samuel J. May Anti-Slavery Movement Collection," Cornell University Library

http://www.nationalgeographic.com/railroad/j1.html
"The Underground Railroad," National Geographic Society

Uncle Tom vs. Blackface Minstrels

Thomas Rice
dressed as Jim Crow

In 1851, the *National Era* began to feature a novel in serial form. It was written by Harriet Beecher Stowe, and it became an instant hit in the North. It was then published in book form and was entitled *Uncle Tom's Cabin, or Life Among the Lowly.*

Mrs. Stowe was the daughter of a famous minister, Lyman Beecher; sister of Reverend Henry Ward Beecher; and wife of Reverend Calvin Stowe. She gained a knowledge of the actual operations of slavery by making a trip into Kentucky, where she and her husband were guests of a plantation owner. She hid runaway slaves in her house in Cincinnati. Then, in 1850, she and her husband moved to Maine, and there, on a dark and gloomy Sunday during church, she saw the image of an African-American man being beaten by two other African-Americans while a white man urged them on. She rushed home and began to write her book.

Except for one, the white characters in the book were good people who were caught up in an evil system. The cruel overseer Simon Legree was a northerner who had moved to the South, and he enjoyed abusing his slaves. When Uncle Tom refused to follow his command to beat a slave woman, Legree turned his two African-American henchmen, Quimbo and Sambo, loose on Uncle Tom. People today describe an African-American who meekly gives in to whites as an "Uncle Tom," but that is a distorted view of Uncle Tom's character. He was stubborn and quietly defiant, refusing to give in to Legree's demands.

On the first day, the book sold 3,000 copies, and by the end of 1852, it had sold 300,000 copies in the United States. In England, it became a bestseller and sold 1.5 million copies. By 1913, the book was available in 66 languages. It had great influence on the events that followed, and Abraham Lincoln credited Mrs. Stowe as being the lady who started the Civil War. The emotional impact of the suffering of Uncle Tom caused many tears to flow by people who had always thought that African-Americans had no feelings.

But if Uncle Tom was creating a sympathetic hearing for African-Americans, some performers in ridiculous costumes, engaging in corny humor, and wearing black makeup, were subjecting them to ridicule. The most popular company was the Christy's Minstrels, the group for whom Stephen Foster wrote many of his songs. Amateur comedians all over the country could easily buy copies of minstrel routines and chuckle at the pretensions of African-Americans trying to rise above their lowly status in life. They appealed especially to immigrants—who were almost as far down the ladder as African-Americans.

The success of minstrels in the North confirmed what Alexis de Tocqueville had written in the 1830s in *Democracy in America.* He wrote that race prejudice was greatest in those states where slavery no longer existed.

RESULTS: The sympathetic view of African-Americans found in *Uncle Tom's Cabin* affected the opinion of many Americans, but a large segment of white Americans found their views of race confirmed by the blackface comedians who caused laughter at the African-Americans' expense.

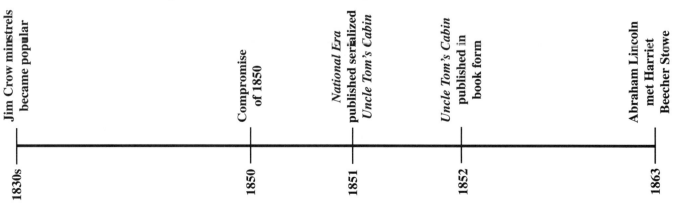

Jim Crow minstrels became popular	Compromise of 1850	*National Era* published serialized *Uncle Tom's Cabin*	*Uncle Tom's Cabin* published in book form	Abraham Lincoln met Harriet Beecher Stowe
1830s	1850	1851	1852	1863

Name: _____ Date: _____

Uncle Tom vs. Blackface Minstrels: Reinforcement

Directions: Complete the following activities, essays, and challenges on your own paper.

ACTIVITIES:

1. Some abolitionist writers quoted newspaper reports about slavery in southern newspapers. Ask the class which approach (a novel or a newspaper report) would most sway them.
2. Discuss the harm that can be done by ridiculing a person or group.

ESSAYS:

1. Do you think a novelist like Mrs. Stowe can make a better case against slavery than a journalist who is limited to the facts he uncovers? Explain.
2. Why do you think a book about American slavery was so popular in other parts of the world?
3. Why is ridicule so harmful to a person or group who is having a difficult time succeeding?

CHALLENGES:

1. What was the full title of Mrs. Stowe's book?
2. What experience had she had with slavery?
3. Who was the cruel overseer in *Uncle Tom's Cabin*?
4. How many copies of Mrs. Stowe's book were sold in the United States?
5. How many copies were sold in England?
6. Who said that Mrs. Stowe started the Civil War?
7. How did minstrel performers dress?
8. Who especially enjoyed minstrel shows?
9. What famous composer wrote music for minstrel shows?
10. What was the most famous minstrel group?

NATIONAL STANDARDS CORRELATIONS:

NCSS Ic: (Culture) Explain and give examples of how language, literature, the arts, architecture, other artifacts, traditions, beliefs, values, and behaviors contribute to the development and transmission of culture.
NSH Era 4, Standard 4: The sources and character of cultural, religious, and social reform movements in the antebellum period

WEBSITES:

http://www.americaslibrary.gov/cgi-bin/page.cgi/jb/reform/beecher_1
"*Uncle Tom's Cabin* Appeared in Serial Form, June 5, 1851," The Library of Congress

http://www.harrietbeecherstowecenter.org/life/#influence
"Harriet's Life & Times," Harriet Beecher Stowe House

http://www.pbs.org/wgbh/amex/foster/sfeature/sf_minstrelsy.html
"Blackface Minstrelsy," Public Broadcasting Service

http://etext.lib.virginia.edu/railton/huckfinn/minstrl.html
"Blackface Minstrelsy," University of Virginia

The Battle Over Kansas

The gold rush of 1849 greatly increased California's population and its awareness that it was very isolated. Mail shipped around South America or overland arrived far too slowly to suit either the sender or receiver. A railroad to California seemed like a likely solution to the problem, but where should it be located? Secretary of War Jefferson Davis sent out a survey team to study a route from New Orleans to California, and when they decided that the best route lay in Mexico's territory, Congress bought the Gadsden Purchase in 1853.

Brooks attacking Sumner with a cane

Many Northerners in Congress wanted the railroad to start in the North, and the new chairman of the Senate Committee on Territories, Stephen Douglas, agreed. If a railroad were to be built, a government would be needed to survey, sell land, and protect railroad right-of-ways. He proposed that a Nebraska Territory be created out of the huge area west of Missouri and north of Iowa. The Missouri Compromise had declared that slavery could not exist in that region, but southerners wanted the rules changed. After pressure from President Pierce and the South, Douglas changed his proposal. There would be two territories created: Kansas and Nebraska.

Added to the proposal was a statement allowing slavery—*if* the settlers wanted it. Known as "popular sovereignty," the right of choice seemed democratic, but both sides were determined to win by any means. Senator David Atchison of Missouri recruited southerners to settle in Kansas; anti-slavery groups formed the New England Emigrant Aid Company to finance northern settlers wanting to move to Kansas. In 1855, the first election was held in Kansas, and thousands of pro-slave Missourians crossed into Kansas to vote. A pro-slave legislature was set up at Lecompton, but the anti-slavery people formed a government of their own at Topeka. Many Americans were disgusted when Pierce supported the southern legislature, and that led to formation of the Republican party.

New terms were being used. A *doughface* was a northern politician who gave in to southern demands. A *free soiler* was a person who did not mind slavery in the South, but did not want slavery to expand into the territories.

Violence led to the nickname of "Bleeding Kansas." A pro-slave mob attacked Lawrence, Kansas, and burned much of the town. An abolitionist, John Brown, led an attack on a slave community and brutally murdered five men. After Senator Charles Sumner gave his "Crime Against Kansas" speech, in which he insulted certain members of Congress, Preston Brooks, a member of the House, beat Sumner with a cane in the Senate chamber. Twenty years before, the House had tried to silence anti-slavery forces with the "gag rule," but now slavery was Congress's most discussed topic.

RESULTS: Slavery was dividing the country, and people feared it might lead to a war. Some hoped that the choice of Democratic candidate James Buchanan, a doughface, would calm everyone down.

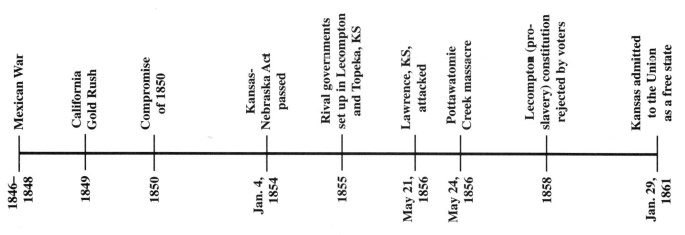

Mexican War	California Gold Rush	Compromise of 1850	Kansas-Nebraska Act passed	Rival governments set up in Lecompton and Topeka, KS	Lawrence, KS, attacked	Pottawatomie Creek massacre	Lecompton (pro-slavery) constitution rejected by voters	Kansas admitted to the Union as a free state
1846–1848	1849	1850	Jan. 4, 1854	1855	May 21, 1856	May 24, 1856	1858	Jan. 29, 1861

Name: _____ Date: _____

The Battle Over Kansas: Reinforcement

Directions: Complete the following activities, essays, and challenges on your own paper.

ACTIVITIES:

1. Have class members write statements expressing the free soiler, abolitionist, or doughface viewpoint, and let others guess which side they chose.
2. In 1856, northerners and southerners argued that it was the other side that had caused the trouble. Have members of the class argue over who was at fault.

ESSAYS:

1. Explain how a railroad to California led to a debate over slavery.
2. What was the connection between the formation of the Republican Party and the slavery issue?
3. Very few slaves were ever taken into Kansas. Why?

CHALLENGES:

1. Why did the United States want to acquire the Gadsden Purchase?
2. Who was chairman of the Senate Committee on Territories?
3. What two territories did Douglas suggest be formed in the West?
4. What purpose would the new territories serve?
5. Which side did Pierce favor?
6. What two legislatures were formed in Kansas, and which group did each represent?
7. If a northern politician was willing to give in to southern demands, what nickname was given to him?
8. What was a person called who wanted slavery kept out of the territories?
9. What town in Kansas was attacked by pro-slavery men?
10. What person was beaten with a cane in the Senate chamber?

NATIONAL STANDARDS CORRELATIONS:

NCSS VIc: (Power, Authority, & Governance) Analyze and explain ideas and governmental mechanisms to meet needs and wants of citizens, regulate territory, manage conflict, and establish order and security.
NSH Era 5, Standard 1: The causes of the Civil War

WEBSITES:

http://memory.loc.gov/ammem/today/apr23.html
"Today in History: April 23," The Library of Congress

http://www.pbs.org/wgbh/aia/part4/4p2952.html
"Bleeding Kansas: 1853–1861," Public Broadcasting Service

http://www.kancoll.org/galbks.htm
"Bleeding Kansas," Kansas Collection

http://lincoln.lib.niu.edu/biography6text.html
"The Kansas-Nebraska Act and the Rise of the Republican Party, 1854–1856," Abraham Lincoln Historical Digitization Project

Courts, Debates, and Attacks

Dred Scott

In 1857, the Supreme Court handed down its long-awaited ruling in the case of *Dred Scott v. Sandford.* Scott had been the slave of an army doctor and had traveled with him to Illinois (a free state) and Minnesota (a free territory). After the master died, Scott sued for his freedom in Missouri courts, arguing that his residence in free areas entitled him to become a free man. The case went to the U.S. Supreme Court where Chief Justice Roger Taney handed down the majority decision. Taney ruled that (1) African-Americans could not be citizens of the United States because when the Constitution was adopted, they were "so far inferior that they had no rights which a white man was bound to respect," and (2) the Missouri Compromise was unconstitutional because it denied the right of an American citizen to take his slave property into the territories.

Northern African-Americans were not surprised by the ruling; they said it confirmed the government's policy from the beginning. Frederick Douglass saw some hope that it would arouse the "National Conscience" of white public opinion. White southerners praised the court for its wisdom, but northerners were quick to attack it. Abolitionists and free soilers were especially angry, and their mass rallies and editorials blasted the Court.

The next year, Stephen Douglas's term in the Senate was up, and the Illinois legislature would vote on whether to keep him or replace him with the Republicans' choice, Abraham Lincoln. As author of the Kansas-Nebraska Act and a believer in popular sovereignty, Douglas had clashed with President Buchanan, who had sided with the phony Lecompton legislature in Kansas. Lincoln was an able lawyer and politician who looked for ways in which to weaken Douglas. Lincoln suggested that they hold debates, and Douglas accepted.

At Freeport, Lincoln asked if the people of a territory could keep slavery out, and Douglas responded with what became known as the "Freeport Doctrine." Douglas said they could keep it out by not passing laws to protect slave property. With Democrats in the new legislature outnumbering Republicans, Douglas was chosen; however, Lincoln had become famous.

In the mind of John Brown, slaves were never going to be freed until a major blow was struck. Gathering a few men together, he planned to capture the federal arsenal at Harpers Ferry, Virginia. He would free the slaves in the area and, using the mountains as a shield, move down the Appalachians, building an army as he went. Attacking on October 16, 1859, he captured the town for a while, but it did not take long for militia and marines to be sent there. Brown and his men were surrounded by a force led by Colonel Robert E. Lee; he was captured, tried, and executed.

RESULTS: The white South feared that "reasonable men" like Taney were few in number in the North, and they feared that Republicans like Lincoln were quickly becoming the majority. If that was true, they would have no choice except to leave the Union.

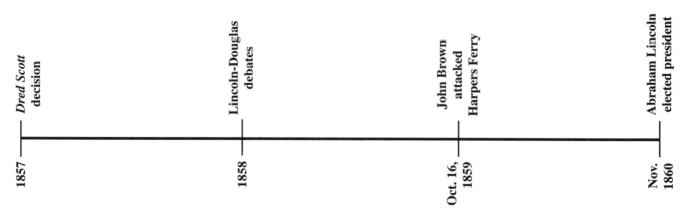

Dred Scott decision — 1857

Lincoln-Douglas debates — 1858

John Brown attacked Harpers Ferry — Oct. 16, 1859

Abraham Lincoln elected president — Nov. 1860

Name: _____ Date: _____

Courts, Debates, and Attacks: Reinforcement

Directions: Complete the following activities, essays, and challenges on your own paper.

ACTIVITIES:

1. Discuss how the *Dred Scott* decision appeared to African-Americans after the Civil War.
2. After bringing in more facts about the life of John Brown, ask if the class thinks he was evil, crazy, or a martyr for the abolition cause.

ESSAYS:

1. How would you react to the *Dred Scott* decision as a free African-American, a Southern white, or a free soiler?
2. Douglas lost southern support for his effort to become president. Why?
3. Why do you think free African-Americans like Frederick Douglass refused to go with John Brown on his raid?

CHALLENGES:

1. Why did Dred Scott think he should be freed?
2. Who handed down the majority decision in *Dred Scott v. Sandford?*
3. What were two important points made by the majority in the *Dred Scott* case?
4. How did Frederick Douglass react to the decision?
5. Who opposed Stephen Douglas in the 1858 Senate race in Illinois?
6. What position did Douglas take in the Freeport Doctrine?
7. Who was chosen for the U.S. Senate?
8. Why did John Brown pick Harpers Ferry as the place to begin?
9. How did Brown hope to free the South's slaves?
10. What happened to Brown?

NATIONAL STANDARDS CORRELATIONS:

NCSS Xg: (Civil Ideals & Practices) Analyze the influence of diverse forms of public opinion on the development of public policy and decision-making.
NSH Era 5, Standard 1: The causes of the Civil War

WEBSITES:

http://www.loc.gov/rr/program/bib/ourdocs/DredScott.html
"Dred Scott v. Sandford," The Library of Congress

http://memory.loc.gov/ammem/sthtml/sthome.html
"Slaves and the Courts: 1740–1860," The Library of Congress

http://memory.loc.gov/cgi-bin/ampage?collId=mfd&fileName=21/21039/21039page.db&recNum=24
"Two Speeches by Frederick Douglass; West India Emancipation…And the Dred Scott Decision," The Library of Congress

http://www.sos.mo.gov/archives/resources/africanamerican/scott/scott.asp
"Missouri's Dred Scott Case, 1846–1857," Missouri State Archives

African-Americans Agitate for Freedom

When Lincoln was elected in 1860, the South seceded from the Union. Beginning with South Carolina in December 1860, seven states of the Deep South left the Union to form the Confederate States of America (CSA). After the attack on Ft. Sumter in Charleston Harbor, four more slave states left the Union (Virginia, Tennessee, Arkansas, and North Carolina). However, four key slave states were still in the Union (Missouri, Kentucky, Maryland, and Delaware), and Lincoln did not want to do anything that might cause them to join the others. Besides, many northerners, especially Democrats and poor immigrants, opposed freeing slaves. If he moved too quickly, he would lose their support for the war.

Lincoln was also troubled by the Constitution's requirement that no property may be taken by government without just compensation (Amendment V). Lincoln had always opposed slavery and called it "an unqualified evil to the Negro, to the white man, and to the State." Now, as president, he seemed to drag his heels, and he waited for public opinion to come around.

Rev. James Pennington

African-Americans were critical of Lincoln. Harriet Tubman declared, "God won't let Mister Lincoln beat the South until he does the right thing." Reverend James W. C. Pennington said slavery caused the war, and peace could not come until slavery was removed. Frederick Douglass thought that fighting slaveholders without fighting slavery was a "half-hearted business." African-Americans were anxious to end slavery and eager to help fight.

Army officers also put pressure on Lincoln. Three slaves used to build Confederate defenses in Virginia escaped to Union lines, and General Ben Butler refused to return them to their masters. Butler called them "contraband of war," and afterward, runaways were often referred to as "contrabands." General John C. Frémont angered many white Missourians by ordering that slaves of Confederate sympathizers be seized. Lincoln told him that his policy must conform with that established by Congress.

Policy was not in Lincoln's hand alone. Congress wrestled with the issue as well. Congress passed the Crittenden-Johnson Resolution in 1861, which said the war was only to preserve the Union. In January 1862, a law was passed forbidding army officers from returning slaves to masters. In April 1862, slavery was outlawed in the District of Columbia; masters received $300 as compensation. In June, it outlawed slavery in the territories. In July, Congress passed the second Confiscation Act, which said that slaves escaping to Union lines "shall be forever free."

By that time, Lincoln had also decided to act; but, following the advice of Secretary of State Seward, he waited until after the North had won a major battle at Antietam to announce his Emancipation Proclamation.

RESULTS: The Emancipation Proclamation gave freedom only to slaves in Confederate hands as of January 1, 1863. The prayers of African-Americans were on their way to being answered. When the Thirteenth Amendment was adopted, the "day of jubilee" came for all.

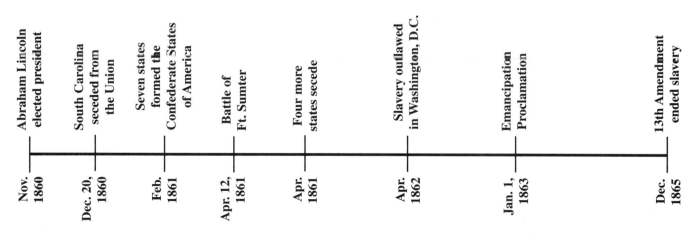

Abraham Lincoln elected president	South Carolina seceded from the Union	Seven states formed the Confederate States of America	Battle of Ft. Sumter	Four more states secede	Slavery outlawed in Washington, D.C.	Emancipation Proclamation	13th Amendment ended slavery
Nov. 1860	Dec. 20, 1860	Feb. 1861	Apr. 12, 1861	Apr. 1861	Apr. 1862	Jan. 1, 1863	Dec. 1865

Name: _____ Date: _____

African-Americans Agitate for Freedom: Reinforcement

Directions: Complete the following activities, essays, and challenges on your own paper.

ACTIVITIES:

1. Examine a map showing the four slave states still in the Union, discuss whether Lincoln was right in being concerned about what would happen if they seceded.
2. Have students read the Emancipation Proclamation and ask for their comments. Was it the dramatic document for which the slaves had been looking?

ESSAYS:

1. You have been called on to defend the ending of slavery as a "military necessity." How would you answer?
2. What risks did Lincoln take in freeing slaves?
3. What risks would Lincoln have taken if he had freed no slaves?

CHALLENGES:

1. How many states joined the CSA altogether?
2. How many slave states remained in the Union?
3. What large groups in the North did not want to free slaves?
4. Who called slavery "an unqualified evil"?
5. Name three African-Americans critical of Lincoln's slow movement toward emancipation.
6. What nickname did General Butler give runaways from slavery?
7. What was General Frémont's policy that angered Missourians?
8. How many slaves were to be freed by the Crittenden-Johnson resolution?
9. What slaves were freed by the second Confiscation Act?
10. What slaves were to be freed by the Emancipation Proclamation?

NATIONAL STANDARDS CORRELATIONS:

NCSS Xf: (Civic Ideals & Practices) Identify and explain the roles of formal and informal political actors in influencing and shaping public policy and decision-making.
NSH Era 5, Standard 2: The course and character of the Civil War and its effects on the American people

WEBSITES:

http://www.loc.gov/rr/program/bib/ourdocs/EmanProc.html
"Emancipation Proclamation," The Library of Congress

http://memory.loc.gov/ammem/alhtml/malhome.html
"Abraham Lincoln Papers," The Library of Congress

http://memory.loc.gov/ammem/aaohtml/exhibit/aopart4.html
"The Civil War," The Library of Congress

African-Americans Fight For Freedom

54th Massachusetts Infantry

From the beginning of the Civil War, African-Americans in the North and South offered to volunteer for military service. The **South** was nervous about how slaves would react to the war; some went to war as body servants to their masters, and others worked faithfully on plantations and farms. Most slaves, however, saw the war as their chance at freedom. Rather than risk getting caught by patrollers, they stayed on the farm and did as little work as possible, waiting for blue uniforms to appear on the horizon. When the right moment came, they joined a long procession of contrabands.

Slaves were used to build defenses and as teamsters, mechanics, and industrial workers. With the war going badly for the South, General Patrick Cleburne suggested in 1864 that African-American units be organized on the promise of freedom after the war. The idea was rejected, but in March 1865 General Robert E. Lee endorsed it as a necessary move. The bill passed in the Confederate Congress, but it was too late to help. The war was nearly over.

The **North** moved slowly toward a policy, fearing that border state support would be lost if African-American troops were enrolled. Before emancipation, the South used its African-American population more effectively than the Union. With enlistments running out and few whites volunteering, the North began to draft soldiers, while African-Americans eagerly wanted to enlist. By autumn 1862, Lincoln allowed African-American units to be organized. In 1863, General Lorenzo Thomas was sent to recruit African-American troops in the Mississippi Valley. Designated as "United States Colored Troops," their units were commanded by white officers. Some officers with long abolitionist backgrounds were eager to command these units, including Thomas Higginson and Robert Shaw.

In comparison with white troops, African-Americans were treated badly. White privates received $13 a month and $3.50 for clothing, but African-Americans were paid $7 a month with a $3 clothing allowance. African-American soldiers in the 54th Massachusetts Infantry refused to accept their pay on this discriminatory basis. In 1864, the pay of African-American soldiers was raised to a level equal with whites.

Although African-Americans participated in many other battles, two particularly stand out. At Ft. Pillow, Tennessee, the Union army was defeated; but when African-American soldiers tried to surrender, Confederates kept firing until more than 100 were killed. African-American prisoners were returned to their masters or put to work on building Confederate defenses.

The most dramatic event involving African-American troops was the attack by the 54th Massachusetts Infantry on Ft. Wagner in 1863. In that attack, 247 men were killed out of the 600 men in the regiment. In battle, African-Americans proved that they deserved the status of free men.

RESULTS: The declining African-American support for the war helped cripple the South's war effort. On the other hand, the African-American soldiers' enthusiasm for a chance to prove themselves in combat earned them more respect than they had ever received before.

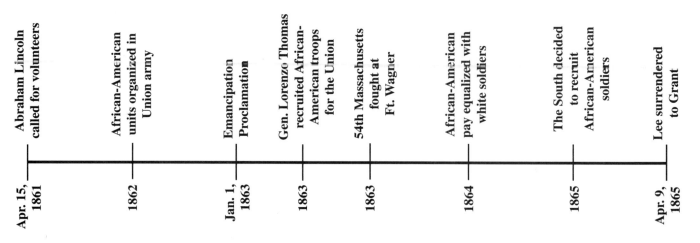

Abraham Lincoln called for volunteers	African-American units organized in Union army	Emancipation Proclamation	Gen. Lorenzo Thomas recruited African-American troops for the Union	54th Massachusetts fought at Ft. Wagner	African-American pay equalized with white soldiers	The South decided to recruit African-American soldiers	Lee surrendered to Grant
Apr. 15, 1861	1862	Jan. 1, 1863	1863	1863	1864	1865	Apr. 9, 1865

Name: _____ Date: _____

African-Americans Fight For Freedom: Reinforcement

Directions: Complete the following activities, essays, and challenges on your own paper.

ACTIVITIES:

1. Have a class debate on the subject: should the North recruit African-American troops?
2. Since the South would not exchange African-American prisoners, ask the class if they think Lincoln was right to refuse to exchange any prisoners.

ESSAYS:

1. Reacting as a southern slave, what would you be thinking as the Union army neared your plantation?
2. If you were a southern supporter of using African-American troops and promising them freedom if they volunteered, what kinds of criticism would you get?
3. As a Northern white, argue in favor of or against using African-American troops in 1863.

CHALLENGES:

1. Did most slaves escape to freedom after the Emancipation Proclamation was announced?
2. Who first suggested that the Confederacy use African-American troops?
3. Who organized African-American regiments for the Union in the Mississippi Valley?
4. Name two officers commanding African-American troops.
5. What was the total pay (including clothing allowances) for Union soldiers, white and African-American?
6. When was the pay for white and African-American soldiers equalized?
7. Why was the Battle of Ft. Pillow later called "a massacre"?
8. What losses did the 54th Massachusetts Infantry suffer at Ft. Wagner?
9. Was the South helped or hurt by African-American behavior toward the end of the war?
10. How did African-Americans earn special respect during the war?

NATIONAL STANDARDS CORRELATIONS:

NCSS IIc: (Time, Continuity, & Change) Identify and describe selected historical periods and patterns of change within and across cultures, such as the rise of civilizations, the development of transportation systems, the growth and breakdown of colonial systems, and others.
NSH Era 5, Standard 2: The course and character of the Civil War and its effects on the American People

WEBSITES:

http://www.archives.gov/education/lessons/blacks-civil-war/
"Teaching With Documents: The Fight for Equal Rights: Black Soldiers in the Civil War," The U.S. National Archives and Records Administration

http://memory.loc.gov/ammem/ndlpedu/features/timeline/civilwar/aasoldrs/soldiers.html
"Civil War and Reconstruction: 1861–1877: African-American Soldiers During the Civil War," The Library of Congress

http://www.itd.nps.gov/cwss/history/aa_history.htm
"History of African-Americans in the Civil War," National Park Service

The Road To Freedom

It happened just as the slaves dreamed it would—a Union officer rode up to the plantation and informed the slaves they were now free by order of the Emancipation Proclamation. The "day of jubilee" had finally come, and the freedmen celebrated. Bonfires were built, hats were tossed in the air, and dancing followed far into the night. By dawn, the fires were burned out, the hats lay on the ground, and the dancing had stopped. This was the day after the party, and reality was beginning to set in.

Many slaves wrapped up their few belongings and took off. Some went in search of long-lost relatives: husbands looking for wives, parents for children, brothers for sisters. Once located, husbands and wives went to a minister to say their vows—this time "'til death us do part."

This was the beginning of the time known as *Reconstruction.* For both races, these were hard times. Much of the South had been destroyed: railroad rails were wrapped around trees, barns had been dismantled for firewood, and homes had been looted. Fields had been neglected and were overgrown with weeds. There were few horses and mules with which to work, but the plows and harnesses were gone anyway. People subsisted on little more than air and water.

In Washington, there was also uncertainty. Coming into power when Congress was adjourned, Vice President Andrew Johnson succeeded the murdered Lincoln. A southerner himself, Johnson had grown up hating the wealthy plantation owners, and he blamed them for starting the war. He wanted to give self-government back to the states as quickly as possible. He required only that qualified southerners sign a loyalty oath, and all property except slaves would be returned. When enough had signed, the oath takers could form conventions and begin governing themselves.

The restored governments began to follow policies sure to arouse the anger of the North. (1) They abolished slavery, but let it be known it was only because of federal government pressure. (2) They elected former Confederate military and civil officers to Congress and high state positions. (3) Gangs of white thugs starting race riots became common. (4) States passed the Black Codes to replace the old slave codes. Some provisions were necessary: make slave marriages legal, give African-Americans the right to own property, to testify in cases involving other African-Americans, and to make contracts.

It was in the restrictions that African-American rights were threatened. The codes varied from one state to another, but the more common provisions included: they were not to keep firearms, intermarry with whites, testify against whites, fail to live up to the letter of contracts, or enter certain trades. If they did not have a job, they could be fined for vagrancy and rented out by the sheriff until the fine was worked off.

RESULTS: Until Congress stepped in, African-Americans were little better off than they had been under slavery. What was clear was southern refusal to give up any more white authority over African-Americans than was absolutely necessary.

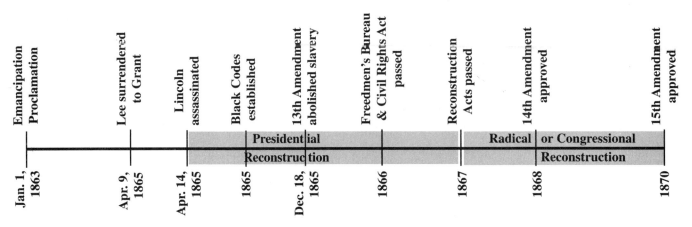

Emancipation Proclamation	Lee surrendered to Grant	Lincoln assassinated	Black Codes established	13th Amendment abolished slavery	Freedmen's Bureau & Civil Rights Act passed	Reconstruction Acts passed	14th Amendment approved	15th Amendment approved
			Presidential Reconstruction			Radical or Congressional Reconstruction		
Jan. 1, 1863	Apr. 9, 1865	Apr. 14, 1865	1865	Dec. 18, 1865	1866	1867	1868	1870

Name: _____ Date: _____

The Road To Freedom: Reinforcement

Directions: Complete the following activities, essays, and challenges on your own paper.

ACTIVITIES:

1. Have the students make a list of jobs that needed to be done in the South after the war. Ask why African-Americans were very important in getting the South on the mend.
2. As a northern abolitionist, decide how you would react to the various provisions of the Black Codes.

ESSAYS:

1. Why were the vagrancy provisions of the Black Codes especially threatening to freedpersons?
2. As a Southern white, why would you be irritated in April and May of 1865 when African-Americans left your farm to look for lost relatives?
3. As a freedman, how would you answer the complaints of Southern white farmers?

CHALLENGES:

1. What was meant by the "day of jubilee"?
2. What problems faced southern farmers after the war?
3. Who replaced Lincoln as president?
4. In the first part of Reconstruction, who would be allowed to vote?
5. When could conventions be formed in the South to draft new constitutions?
6. Who usually started race riots?
7. What laws did the Black Codes replace?
8. Under the Black Codes, in what kinds of cases could African-Americans testify?
9. What parts of the Black Codes limited African-American economic activity?
10. If an African-American were unemployed (vagrant), what would happen when he could not pay his fine?

NATIONAL STANDARDS CORRELATIONS:

NCSS VId: (Power, Authority, & Governance) Describe the ways nations and organizations respond to forces of unity and diversity affecting order and security.
NSH Era 5, Standard 3: How various Reconstruction plans succeeded or failed

WEBSITES:

http://memory.loc.gov/ammem/aapchtml/aapchome.html
"From Slavery to Freedom: The African-American Pamphlet Collection, 1822–1909," The Library of Congress

http://www.tsha.utexas.edu/handbook/online/articles/FF/ncfl.html
"Freedmen's Bureau," The Texas State Historical Association

http://www.history.umd.edu/Freedmen/
"Freedmen and Southern Society Project," University of Maryland

Reconstruction

Senator Blanche Bruce

After Lincoln's assassination in April 1865, Vice President Andrew Johnson became president, and he restored civil government to the South. When Congress returned in December 1865, it expressed its anger with the president's program. Most of the group later known as Radical Republicans had long anti-slavery records and included Thaddeus Stevens in the House and Charles Sumner in the Senate. In their view, the South had lost its status in the Union and could return only when it gave African-Americans full and equal rights. Most in Congress were willing, at first, to try and work with Johnson. That attitude began to change after he vetoed the Freedmen's Bureau bill and the Civil Rights bill. Congress passed the bills over his veto, and the Radicals became more vocal. The 1866 election returned so many Radicals that they could override any presidential veto.

The Reconstruction Act passed in 1867; it created military rule for the ten unreconstructed southern states and a new loyalty oath that disfranchised (took away the vote) from most white voters. In those ten states, African-American voters outnumbered whites, and far more African-Americans were Republican than Democrat. Some of the whites were northerners, who were labelled *carpetbaggers*. Others were native southerners, mostly former Whigs, who were called *scalawags*. Working to get African-Americans to vote were Freedmen's Bureau agents and members of the Union League, a Republican group formed during the war to stir support for Lincoln.

Many stereotypes remain about the governments created in the South after the Civil War. (1) *These governments were dominated by African-Americans.* In reality, only two African-Americans became senators, 20 went to the House from 1869–1901, none became governors, and only the South Carolina lower House had an African-American majority. (2) *The people who ran these governments were ignorant, former slaves.* Those who became leaders had been free African-Americans before the war, and some had been educated in the North or in England. Their strong support for public school systems indicated a deep interest in education. (3) *The governments they created were corrupt.* There is no denying that power corrupts, and people are vulnerable. These legislatures ran up debts of $305 million by 1871. Some states wasted large amounts, but much of the expense was in building needed schools, roads, and railroads.

Southern whites resisted what seemed an "unnatural situation," with African-Americans writing the rules. Terrorist organizations like the Ku Klux Klan developed to keep "uppity blacks" in their place, and the group also went after Union Leaguers, Yankee school teachers, Freedmen's Bureau agents, carpetbaggers, and the scalawags who encouraged them.

RESULTS: In 1877, the last Reconstruction governments fell, and government was returned to the states. For African-Americans, it was a hard civics lesson, but easy progress has rarely been part of the African-American experience.

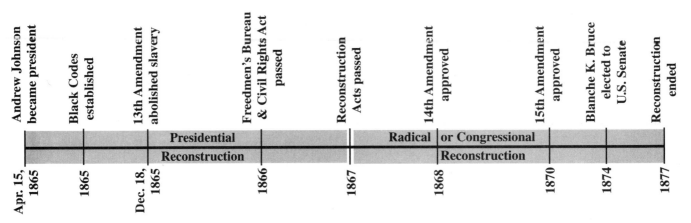

Andrew Johnson became president	Black Codes established	13th Amendment abolished slavery	Freedmen's Bureau & Civil Rights Act passed	Reconstruction Acts passed	14th Amendment approved	15th Amendment approved	Blanche K. Bruce elected to U.S. Senate	Reconstruction ended
		Presidential Reconstruction			Radical or Congressional Reconstruction			
Apr. 15, 1865	1865	Dec. 18, 1865	1866	1867	1868	1870	1874	1877

Name: _____ Date: _____

Reconstruction: Reinforcement

Directions: Complete the following activities, essays, and challenges on your own paper.

ACTIVITIES:

1. Ask why the class feels that more African-Americans were *not* elected, especially since they were the majority of qualified voters.
2. Ask the class how Reconstruction could have had a better result.

ESSAYS:

1. As a scalawag, you have been criticized by former friends for having sold out. How would you respond?
2. Do you think the terms desired by Radical Republicans in 1867 had been completely met by 1877?
3. As a freedman who had lived through the entire period, how would you feel about the experience in 1877?

CHALLENGES:

1. Who were the Radical Republican leaders?
2. What caused Johnson to lose support in Congress?
3. What were two major provisions of the Reconstruction Act?
4. What name was given to northerners who moved to the South and supported Reconstruction government?
5. What name was given to southern supporters of Reconstruction?
6. How many African-Americans were elected to the Senate and House in the nineteenth century?
7. How did African-American legislators feel about schools?
8. What were important expenditures of Reconstruction governments?
9. What was the best-known terrorist group?
10. What groups did the terrorist group target?

NATIONAL STANDARDS CORRELATIONS:

<u>**NCSS IVg:**</u> (Individual Development & Identity) Identify and interpret examples of stereotyping, conformity, and altruism.
<u>**NSH Era 5, Standard 3:**</u> How various Reconstruction plans succeeded or failed

WEBSITES:

http://memory.loc.gov/ammem/aaohtml/exhibit/aopart5.html
"Reconstruction and Its Aftermath," The Library of Congress

http://www.pbs.org/wgbh/amex/reconstruction/
"Reconstruction: The Second Civil War," Public Broadcasting Service

http://blackhistory.harpweek.com/4Reconstruction/ReconLevelOne.htm
"Toward Racial Equality: Harper's Weekly Reports on Black America, 1857–1874," HarpWeek

http://www.digitalhistory.uh.edu/reconstruction/section1/section1_intro.html
"A New Birth of Freedom: Reconstruction During the Civil War," Digital History

From Slavery to Sharecropping

Slaves owned very little, but they dreamed that when the "day of jubilee" came, they would earn some money, buy land and a couple of mules, and build a house. During Reconstruction, stories spread that the government was going to give them "40 acres and a mule," but when southerners were granted pardons, their property was restored.

Sharecropper Farmhouses

A few African-Americans were fortunate enough to receive land or buy it on very reasonable terms. General Rufus Saxton tried to divide plantations into smaller units and give African-Americans the opportunity to buy them, but the Treasury Department sold most of it to whites who had the cash to pay off back taxes. General Sherman set aside land for African-Americans on the offshore islands, and some of Jefferson Davis's slaves bought part of his Mississippi plantation.

The vast majority still worked for a white farmer. In the early days of Reconstruction, if the African-American worker felt he was not being treated fairly under the terms of his contract with the employer and did not receive justice in state court, he could appeal to the Freedmen's United States Courts presided over by a Freedmen's Bureau agent. More often than not, the agent ruled in favor of the freedman.

The system used at first was a gang-labor method. Workers were sent in groups with a white supervisor on horseback watching them. To the African-Americans, this seemed like slavery, and since landowners did not like to pay wages anyway, new approaches were developed.

One was the *sharecrop* system. In it, the landowner provided a house, land, seed, fertilizer, and supplies, and when the crop came in, landowner and "cropper" split the money. The cropper often owed a debt to the landlord for food and other necessities. When the crop came in, that debt had to be repaid with interest. Croppers often got nothing for their labor.

A *tenant farmer* put up everything except land, and for its use, he gave the owner money or part of the crop. It was common for him to pay part in cash plus a third of the crop.

The *crop-lien* system was also common. It was a business arrangement between the farmer and a merchant. The merchant provided food, seed, and other supplies to the farmer in return for a lien (mortgage) on the crop. When it was sold, the merchant was paid first, and whatever was left went to the farmer. Often, he ended up more deeply in debt.

Laws were strict regarding the obligation of debtors; unless all debts were paid in full, the debtor must remain on the land. Booker T. Washington said that sharecropping was as bad as slavery, and using debt to keep a man in place robbed him of independence until he was lost and bewildered.

RESULTS: African-American hopes of economic independence were being crushed by a system that barely stood above the Thirteenth Amendment's definition of slavery, as well as federal laws that made peonage (debt slavery) legal.

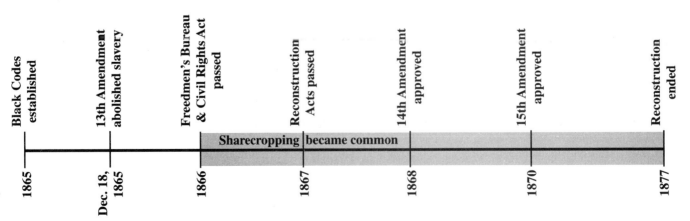

Black Codes established	13th Amendment abolished slavery	Freedmen's Bureau & Civil Rights Act passed	Reconstruction Acts passed	14th Amendment approved	15th Amendment approved	Reconstruction ended
		Sharecropping became common				
1865	Dec. 18, 1865	1866	1867	1868	1870	1877

Name: _____ Date: _____

From Slavery to Sharecropping: Reinforcement

Directions: Complete the following activities, essays, and challenges on your own paper.

ACTIVITIES:

1. Have the class write a skit featuring a discussion between a landowner and a tenant farmer taking place after the crop was sold.
2. Ask the class why laws were so strict on the payment of debt.

ESSAYS:

1. How would you compare sharecropping with slavery?
2. As a landowner, write your opinion of croppers and tenants.
3. As a cropper, write your opinion of the landowner.

CHALLENGES:

1. What rumor was "music to the ears" of freedmen?
2. Who set aside land for freedmen on offshore islands?
3. If they were not satisfied with the verdict in state court, where could freedmen go to appeal?
4. Why didn't African-Americans like the gang-labor approach?
5. What was the usual split between a cropper and landowner?
6. Why did croppers often end up with nothing?
7. After paying part of his rent in cash, how much did a tenant farmer usually have to give out of the crop?
8. Under the crop-lien system, with whom did the farmer sign the lien (mortgage)?
9. Why didn't croppers and others move away?
10. With what did Booker T. Washington compare cropping?

NATIONAL STANDARDS CORRELATIONS:

NCSS VIIf: (Production, Distribution, & Consumption) Explain and illustrate how values and beliefs influence different economic decisions.
NSH Era 5, Standard 3: How various Reconstruction plans succeeded or failed

WEBSITES:

http://www.digitalhistory.uh.edu/reconstruction/section3/section3_intro.html
"From Slave Labor to Free Labor: Introduction," Digital History

http://www.pbs.org/itvs/homecoming/history1.html
"Reconstruction (1866–1877) and Beyond," Public Broadcasting Service

http://teachingamericanhistory.org/library/index.asp?document=545
"Forty Acres and a Mule: Special Field Order No. 15," Ashbrook Center for Public Affairs at Ashland University

Cowboys, Exodusters, and Soldiers

Benjamin "Pap" Singleton

Rising racial tension and hard times in the postwar period caused some African-Americans to take Horace Greeley's advice to go West. In the West, African-American faces had always been rare, but explorers like Estevanico and William Clark's slave, York, and fur traders like Jean DeSable and James Beckwourth, and those joining California gold seekers had been there before the war.

Three groups were especially interesting to the modern world. About 5,000 African-Americans who went west became cowboys. The work was hard, and the men were very dependent on each other. Race was not a big issue in the bunkhouse or on the trail. One African-American cowboy, Bill Pickett, added his bit to western legend when he invented bulldogging—taking a steer by the neck and throwing him down. Pickett actually caught the steer by the nose with his teeth!

Fear of white hoodlums who attacked them without provocation made some African-Americans anxious to find isolated areas of the West where they could make a living and form separate communities. Kansas was close enough and had many undersettled areas available. When Kansas officials traveled to Louisiana and met with African-Americans on the banks of the Mississippi River in 1879, they offered free transportation, land, and supplies for their first year if they would migrate.

Two African-American leaders were boosters for the move. Benjamin "Pap" Singleton had escaped slavery and had lived in Canada where African-American communities had done well. The other was Henry Adams, a former slave and Union army soldier who saw the move as a necessary first step to settlement in Liberia. Whites made every effort to block them from escaping, but the "Exodus of 1879" proceeded anyway. Those who left were called Exodusters.

The Exodusters were farmers accustomed to hard work with little reward, but they had no idea how much adjustment was needed to live in Kansas, where wind and cold were plentiful in winter, but water, wood, and good crops were scarce. Of the towns built, only Nicodemus remains.

The postwar army had two jobs: to support Reconstruction and control the West. Poor pay, isolated posts, and dangerous work awaited those who wore the army's blue uniforms. African-American troops formed the 9th and 10th Cavalry and the 24th and 25th Infantry. They were given poor equipment, uniforms, and horses, but they guarded trails, built telegraph lines, and fought alongside white troops. The Cheyenne called them "buffalo soldiers," because of their black kinky hair. Thirty "Seminole Negro Indian Scouts" were recruited in 1870, and four of them received the Medal of Honor.

Among their officers was Lieutenant Henry Flipper, who was the first African-American to graduate from West Point. White officers included Ben Grierson and John J. Pershing. These units continued until 1952, when the army was integrated.

RESULTS: African-Americans who moved west, whether as cowboys, settlers, or soldiers, found that even though they were needed and they worked hard, the equality they wanted was denied them.

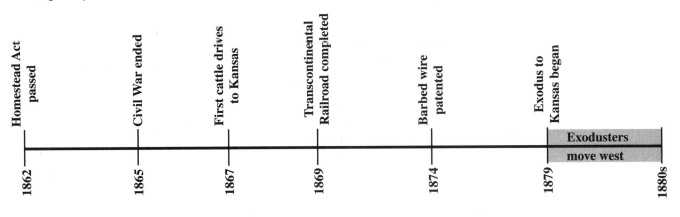

Name: _____   Date: _____

Cowboys, Exodusters, and Soldiers: Reinforcement

Directions: Complete the following activities, essays, and challenges on your own paper.

ACTIVITIES:

1. Read about the geography and climate of Louisiana and Kansas, and make a list of problems the Exodusters might have had in making the transition.
2. Ask the class to rate the three groups (cowboys, Exodusters, and buffalo soldiers) as to (1) financial success, (2) difficulty of work, and (3) a chance to develop independence.

ESSAYS:

1. Farming in Kansas was difficult for any who tried. Looking back, do you think the Exodusters made a mistake? Explain.
2. It is 1879. Write a letter to a friend who is thinking about joining the Exodusters. Should your friend go? Explain why or why not.
3. General Colin Powell is a great fan of Lieutenant Henry Flipper. Read about Flipper and tell why you think he deserves special credit.

CHALLENGES:

1. Who were two early African-American explorers in the West?
2. Name two African-American fur traders.
3. How many African-Americans were cowboys?
4. What sport was invented by African-American cowboy Bill Pickett?
5. What did Kansas offer the Exodusters?
6. Name two African-American boosters of the Exodus.
7. What were the two African-American cavalry regiments? What were the two African-American infantry regiments?
8. Who called the African-American troops "buffalo soldiers," and why?
9. Of the 30 "Seminole Negro Indian Scouts," how many won the medal of honor?
10. Name three well-known officers of buffalo soldiers.

NATIONAL STANDARDS CORRELATIONS:

NCSS IIIh: (People, Places, & Environments) Examine, interpret, and analyze physical and cultural patterns and their interactions, such as land use, settlement patterns, cultural transmission of customs and ideas, and ecosystem changes.

NSH Era 6, Standard 1: How the rise of corporations, heavy industry, and mechanized farming transformed the American people

WEBSITES:

http://www.loc.gov/exhibits/african/afam009.html
"Western Migration and Homesteading," The Library of Congress

http://www.pbs.org/weta/thewest/program/episodes/seven/theexodust.htm
"The Exodusters," Public Broadcasting Service

http://www.tsha.utexas.edu/handbook/online/articles/BB/arb1.html
"Black Cowboys," Texas State Historical Society

African-Americans Head North

Life in the South was growing less secure every day for African-Americans. A number of new problems existed. The slightest violation of any law could have terrible consequences. Convict leasing involved renting out prisoners to private individuals, who abused them badly. At county prison farms, African-American inmates were worked on chain gangs by officials who profited from crops they produced. The officials also pocketed the county's small inmate food allowance. Since these prisons were located in isolated places, the state and public hardly knew they existed.

Lynching (mob action resulting in the death of a person accused of a crime) became common. From 1885–1915, there were 3,500 lynchings; 235 in 1892 alone. Some African-Americans began to think about moving away.

But despite the dangers, many Southern African-Americans had no desire to move away. They had family, friendships, and church ties that were hard to break. There were also economic ties. If they owned their own home and had a job, it was a difficult decision to leave it all behind and venture north.

The newcomers to northern cities found that an African-American community had existed there since colonial times. Some African-Americans had established businesses, owned property, and had done well. Others worked as domestics or day laborers and lived in neighborhoods bearing racially insulting names. Chicago's African-American population grew from 15,000 in 1890 to 50,000 in 1915. It was scattered, but a concentration was forming on the "South Side." White resistance to African-Americans renting or buying property grew at the same time that more space was needed. Landlords realized they could raise rent for African-American tenants, and they would have no choice except to pay. Respectable African-Americans had no control over who moved in next door, and the "Sporting Set" (drifters and the criminal element) became their neighbors.

New York's African-American population began to concentrate on settling in Harlem after the old African-American residential area was torn down to build the Pennsylvania Railroad station and a flood of newcomers poured in from the South. W.E.B. DuBois wrote in 1901 that about one-fourth had good jobs, one-half worked as domestics and day laborers, and the remaining one-fourth lived in poverty.

In New York, Philadelphia, and other northern cities, churches were the most important institutions, with fraternal orders and charitable groups also playing major roles. African-Americans had little contact with whites on the job, in the neighborhood, or in the public schools.

Most white labor unions did not want African-American members—sometimes because of prejudice, but also because employers hired African-Americans as strike breakers. A major exception to discrimination against African-Americans was the Knights of Labor, which had about 65,000 African-American members in 1886. The American Federation of Labor (AFL) was willing to let African-Americans join, but when some craft unions objected, they let each craft union decide its own membership qualifications.

RESULTS: African-Americans found that while more economic opportunities existed in the North, life was hard, and Harlem and the South Side were not Eden.

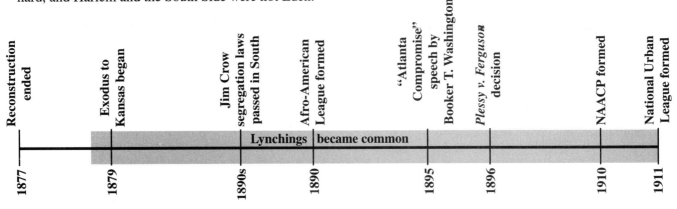

1877	1879	1890s	1890	1895	1896	1910	1911
Reconstruction ended	Exodus to Kansas began	Jim Crow segregation laws passed in South	Afro-American League formed	"Atlanta Compromise" speech by Booker T. Washington	*Plessy v. Ferguson* decision	NAACP formed	National Urban League formed

Lynchings became common

     58

Name: _____ Date: _____

African-Americans Head North: Reinforcement

Directions: Complete the following activities, essays, and challenges on your own paper.

ACTIVITIES:

1. Have the class make a list of reasons why African-Americans should have remained in the South, and why they should have moved to New York.
2. Ask the class to discuss how whites who had lived in Harlem all their lives felt as the population became increasingly African-American.

ESSAYS:

1. Why was the decision to move north difficult for a Southern African-American to make?
2. As an African-American who has gone to Chicago, write a letter to a cousin in the South, telling him or her the pros and cons of city living.
3. Why did African-Americans and whites have little contact in cities? As an African-American of the 1890s, would that have bothered you? Why?

CHALLENGES:

1. What was the system that allowed private individuals to rent out convicts?
2. How did officials at prison farms make money off the prisoners?
3. How many lynchings occurred from 1885–1915?
4. What social ties held African-Americans to the South?
5. How much did Chicago's African-American population grow between 1890 and 1915?
6. Why was rent higher for African-Americans than whites?
7. Why were respectable African-Americans upset by housing conditions?
8. What was the African-American area of Chicago called? What was the African-American area of New York called?
9. What were the important African-American social institutions in the North?
10. Which union discriminated the least against African-Americans?

NATIONAL STANDARDS CORRELATIONS:

NCSS IIIh: (People, Places, & Environments) Examine, interpret, and analyze physical and cultural patterns and their interactions, such as land use, settlement patterns, cultural transmission of customs and ideas, and ecosystem changes.
NSH Era 6, Standard 2: Massive immigration after 1870 and how new social patterns, conflicts, and ideas of national unity developed amid growing cultural diversity

WEBSITES:

http://www.iath.virginia.edu/vcdh/afam/reflector/historicalb.html
"Anti-Lynching Efforts," University of Virginia

http://www.uga.edu/~iaas/Wells.TXT
"Office of Anti-Lynching Bureau," The University of Georgia

http://lcweb.loc.gov/exhibits/african/afam011.html
"Chicago: Destination for the Great Migration," The Library of Congress

Booker T. Washington

Booker T. Washington

Tuskegee, Alabama, was a town with little claim to fame in 1881, when a new principal arrived to take charge of the Tuskegee Normal and Industrial Institute. Chartered by the legislature, with $2,000 appropriated for its first year of operation, it was a school only on paper. By 1895, the school and its leader became nationally known and widely respected. Even then, few could have guessed the influence that the "Tuskegee Machine" would have on African-American affairs for the next 20 years.

Born a slave in Virginia in 1856, Booker T. Washington's mother moved with her children to West Virginia, where Booker worked in a coal mine and attended elementary school. When he was 17, he walked 500 miles to study at Hampton Institute. He needed a job. A teacher told him to clean up a room; he swept it three times and dusted it four times; as a result, he was hired as a janitor. He impressed Superintendent O.K. Armstrong with his intelligence and his positive attitude. When Armstrong was asked to suggest names for the position at Tuskegee, he listed only one: Booker T. Washington.

The African-Americans at Tuskegee were very poor and ignorant. The whites saw no need to educate African-Americans. Their motto was: "Educate a Negro and he won't work." Washington answered that view by requiring that *all* students at Tuskegee *had* to work. He set the example himself. When a wealthy lady saw him walking past, she ordered him to cut wood for her. He took off his coat, cut the wood, and carried it into the kitchen. When a maid told the woman who he was, she was very embarrassed and went to his office. He told her he liked doing favors for his friends. She became a large donor to the school. Other whites soon appreciated the hard-working student body at the school and began employing them.

He made the school as self-sufficient as possible, knowing that the legislature was not generous to African-American schools. In his first five years, he started programs in bricklaying, carpentry, blacksmithing, and farming for the men, and cooking, sewing, and housekeeping for the women.

Pride was also important. Proper speech and dress as well as dignity were required. Students addressed each other with "Mister" and "Miss" and learned proper etiquette. The behavior of students was critical to winning white support.

Washington also won African-American support by speaking in churches and schools. In 1896, the Tuskegee Agricultural Experiment Station opened. Its purpose was to improve African-American farms, and it attracted George Washington Carver to the school. A two-horse vehicle was donated by a New York philanthropist for Carver to use in making field demonstrations. Julius Rosenwald, another wealthy northerner, was also persuaded to fund African-American schools in rural areas, and more than 5,000 African-American schools benefited.

RESULTS: Tuskegee Institute was designed by Washington to change attitudes—the white attitude toward educating African-Americans, and the African-American attitude toward dignity in labor.

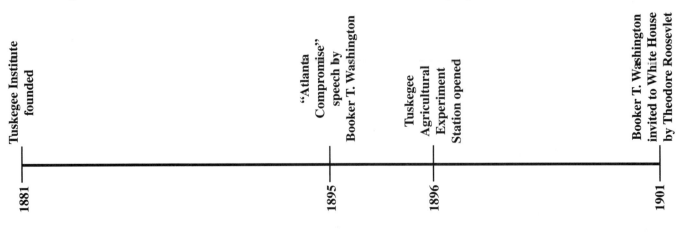

1881	1895	1896	1901
Tuskegee Institute founded	"Atlanta Compromise" speech by Booker T. Washington	Tuskegee Agricultural Experiment Station opened	Booker T. Washington invited to White House by Theodore Roosevelt

Name: _____ Date: _____

Booker T. Washington: Reinforcement

Directions: Complete the following activities, essays, and challenges on your own paper.

ACTIVITIES:

1. Discuss how Washington was able to affect white attitudes toward African-American education by his approach. Ask how students can change negative attitudes that others might have toward them by using his approach.
2. Ask how the class thinks the Tuskegee program received generous support from wealthy northerners.

ESSAYS:

1. How do you think Booker T. Washington's ideas appeared to Alabama whites?
2. If you were an African-American farmer in Alabama, what would you think of the Tuskegee Institute?
3. Why do you think Booker T. Washington was interested in helping African-American public schools in Alabama?

CHALLENGES:

1. How much money did Alabama appropriate for Tuskegee's first year?
2. Where did B.T. Washington receive his college training?
3. Who recommended him for the job at Tuskegee?
4. How did Washington's attitude toward work affect the students at Tuskegee?
5. What kinds of jobs did the men at Tuskegee have?
6. What kind of training did women at Tuskegee receive?
7. What program did he create to help Alabama's farmers?
8. What famous scientist taught at Tuskegee?
9. How did that scientist reach Alabama's farmers?
10. What kind of help did the Rosenwald Fund give to African-Americans?

NATIONAL STANDARDS CORRELATIONS:

NCSS Vc: (Individuals, Groups, & Institutions) Describe the various forms institutions take and the interactions of people with institutions.
NSH Era 6, Standard 1: How the rise of corporations, heavy industry, and mechanized farming transformed the American people

WEBSITES:

http://memory.loc.gov/ammem/aaohtml/exhibit/aopart6.html
"The Booker T. Washington Era," The Library of Congress

http://docsouth.unc.edu/washington/bio.html
"Booker T. Washington, 1856–1915," University Library, The University of North Carolina at Chapel Hill

http://memory.loc.gov/ammem/today/sep18.html
"Today in History: September 18," The Library of Congress

The Disfranchising of African-Americans

turned away from the polls

Poor white farmers were about as numerous as poor African-Americans; if race had not been a factor, the two might have become allies. Hard pressed in competing with large landowners for the sale of their cotton and feeling that the rich used political power for selfish gain, they began to demand changes. Forming the Farmers' Alliance movement in the South and West, they began to pressure both major parties. But when they failed to get control of either one, they developed into the Populist party.

Some southern Populists, like Tom Watson in Georgia, tried to win African-American support. When some African-Americans formed the Colored Farmers' Alliance, their former Democratic allies turned against them. Other Populist leaders, like Ben Tillman and Mississippi's J.K. Vardaman, saw any African-American voter as a threat to white supremacy in the South and wanted to remove African-Americans from the voting lists. They opposed letting *any* African-American vote, even if he was educated or upstanding. They began to look for ways to disfranchise (take the vote away from) African-Americans.

Obstacles stood in the way. The Fifteenth Amendment (1870) clearly stated, "The right ... to vote shall not be denied or abridged ... on account of race, color, or previous condition of servitude." Republican defeats in 1884 and 1892 caused the party to pull away from helping African-Americans to win more white votes. Some in Congress, however, still supported African-American rights.

Disfranchising had to be carried out without mentioning race. One way to accomplish it was the literacy test that would be required of all voters. The questions asked of whites were simple; but African-Americans had questions that would baffle a Supreme Court justice. Senator Henry Blair (R-New Hampshire) offered a bill to provide federal aid to education in 1890, which the South saw as a direct attack on literacy tests and strongly protested. The Blair Bill was defeated, but it was a warning to the South that it must tread carefully.

The poll tax was another approach; it required that all voters pay a tax to cover election costs. Its real purpose was to keep poor whites and African-Americans from voting. The third device was to turn the Democratic party into a "club," and only members could vote in the primary. In the "Solid South," where Democrats ruled supreme, this gave the African-Americans no one for whom to vote in November, even if they had survived all the other restrictions. Senator Henry Cabot Lodge (R-Massachusetts) offered the Force Bill in 1890, which provided for federal monitoring of southern elections. It finally passed the House, but it was too late for the Senate to act.

The effect of disfranchisement was obvious. Alabama had 181,000 African-American voters in 1900, and only 3,000 in 1901. Louisiana's 130,000 registered African-American voters dropped to 1,300 after disfranchisement.

RESULT: When African-Americans lost the vote, they lost any political voice in their state and in national affairs as well. This made it easy to impose new Jim Crow restrictions that pushed them even farther down.

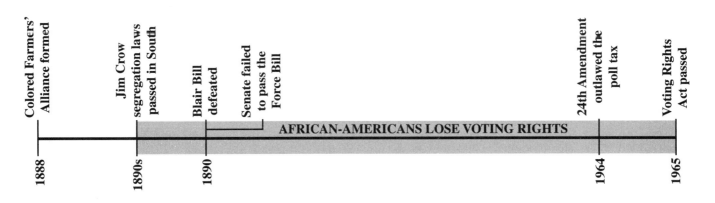

Colored Farmers' Alliance formed — 1888
Jim Crow segregation laws passed in South — 1890s
Blair Bill defeated — 1890
Senate failed to pass the Force Bill
24th Amendment outlawed the poll tax — 1964
Voting Rights Act passed — 1965

AFRICAN-AMERICANS LOSE VOTING RIGHTS

62

Name: _____ Date: _____

The Disfranchising of African-Americans: Reinforcement

Directions: Complete the following activities, essays, and challenges on your own paper.

ACTIVITIES:

1. Discuss the literacy test as a method of determining who could vote. If it were to be brought up before your state legislature this year, which groups would support it, and which would oppose it?
2. Discuss why the right to vote is important to any group. Ask what happens if a group loses the right to vote.

ESSAYS:

1. The "grandfather clause" was included in many states. It provided that if the person or his ancestors could vote in 1867, they were exempt from taking the literacy test and paying special taxes. What do you think was the reason for this?
2. As a supporter of the literacy test and poll tax, what kinds of arguments would you use in their defense?
3. As an opponent of the literacy test and poll tax, what arguments would you use?

CHALLENGES:

1. What movement developed to form the Populist party?
2. Which Populist tried to win African-American support?
3. Which Populists opposed the right of African-Americans to vote?
4. Which Constitutional amendment stood in the way of disfranchisement?
5. Why were Republicans less inclined to help African-Americans than in the past?
6. Why were the literacy tests unfair?
7. Why did the South oppose the Blair Bill?
8. What was the real reason for the poll tax?
9. Why did the Democratic Party become a "club"?
10. Who was author of the Force Bill, and why did it fail to become a law?

NATIONAL STANDARDS CORRELATIONS:

NCSS VIa: (Power, Authority, & Governance) Examine persistent issues involving the rights, roles, and status of the individual in relation to the general welfare.
NSH Era 6, Standard 1: How the rise of corporations, heavy industry, and mechanized farming transformed the American people

WEBSITES:

http://www.iath.virginia.edu.vcdh/afam/politics/home.html
"The Politics of Disfranchisement: White Supremacy & African-American Resistance in Charlottesville, Virginia," University of Virginia

http://www.digitalhistory.uh.edu/database/article_display.cfm?HHID=217
"Segregation and Disfranchisement," Digital History

http://lcweb2.log.gov/ammem/aap/aapmtg.html
"Attend a meeting of the National Afro-American Council," The Library of Congress

"Separate but Equal"

Once the vote was lost, African-Americans were at the mercy of their worst enemies in the South. For the segregationist, it was not enough that the African-American was poor and defenseless; he had to be reminded constantly that he was inferior as well. Jim Crow (segregation) laws were everywhere, and only African-Americans with a death wish ignored them. Informal rules were just as strong, and African-Americans knew that not reacting to a demeaning racial slur was as important as obeying a written law. The Supreme Court had given tacit approval to these social rules when, in the *Civil Rights Cases* (1883), it ruled that the Fourteenth Amendment set limits on what states could do, but *not* on individual acts of discrimination.

Segregated theatre entrance

When Jim Crow moved in, African-Americans drank from separate fountains, used separate restrooms, were limited to the balcony of the theater, and had to sit in the back of the bus. There were separate schools for African-Americans, and these schools had far less tax money support, poor equipment, and lower-paid teachers. Parks and public swimming pools were closed to African-Americans. There were separate state facilities for the insane, blind, deaf, and imprisoned.

The Atlanta Exposition was to be held in 1895, and its leaders asked Booker T. Washington for help in getting federal funding. A Negro Pavilion was included at the Exposition, and Washington was asked to give a speech. He was well aware of: (1) lynchings (He had traveled to many places in the South to cool tensions down.), (2) the desire of some whites in the South to replace African-American workers with immigrants, and (3) the fear of some whites that African-Americans would strike back for the outrages they had suffered.

He was introduced by the governor, and he spoke to the concerns of his audience. He reminded them that African-Americans had always provided a loyal labor core for the South. He urged that the South invest in African-Americans, because "we shall constitute one-third and more of the ignorance and crime of the South, or one-third its intelligence and progress." In a statement that was later criticized by many, he said, "In all things that are purely social we can be as separate as the fingers, yet one as the hand in all things essential to mutual progress." After the speech, the governor shook his hand, and President Cleveland sent a letter of warm congratulations. W.E.B. DuBois and others charged that he had surrendered to white racism.

Homer Plessy, an African-American resident of New Orleans, could not be accused of giving in to Jim Crow. He had boarded a railroad car reserved for whites and refused to give up his seat. The case went to the U.S. Supreme Court as *Plessy v. Ferguson* (1896). The Court said racial separation did not mean either race was inferior, unless "the colored race chooses to put that construction upon it."

RESULTS: Southern African-Americans now faced "separate but equal" doctrine, which allowed them to be cut off from educational and cultural advancement. It became an unfortunate part of everyday life.

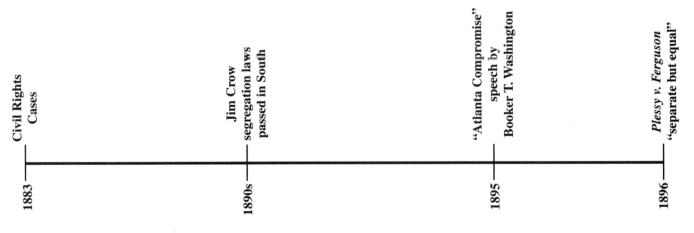

Civil Rights Cases — 1883

Jim Crow segregation laws passed in South — 1890s

"Atlanta Compromise" speech by Booker T. Washington — 1895

Plessy v. Ferguson "separate but equal" — 1896

64

Name: _____ Date: _____

"Separate but Equal": Reinforcement

Directions: Complete the following activities, essays, and challenges on your own paper.

ACTIVITIES:

1. Have the class take an imaginary trip, during which they must obey the formal and informal rules of segregation. Then discuss the way they felt about themselves.
2. Discuss whether Booker T. Washington was acknowledging reality, or whether the class thinks he should have tried to use his platform to attack disfranchisement and segregation.

ESSAYS:

1. As an African-American in the South during segregation, what things that you normally do might be restricted?
2. W.E.B. DuBois and other northern critics felt that B.T. Washington had given up too much with his "Atlanta Compromise" speech. What arguments would you give either attacking or defending that speech?
3. Do you agree with the majority of the Supreme Court, that segregation did not imply inferiority unless African-Americans chose to interpret it that way?

CHALLENGES:

1. By what other name were segregation laws known?
2. Why did the *Civil Rights Cases* decision hurt African-Americans?
3. How were African-American schools discriminated against?
4. What state facilities were segregated?
5. Why was Booker T. Washington concerned about African-Americans losing jobs?
6. Did Booker T. Washington demand social equality in the speech?
7. Who praised the "Atlanta Compromise" speech?
8. Who was critical of it and why?
9. What did Plessy do that got him into trouble?
10. In the eyes of the majority on the Supreme Court, did segregation mean that African-Americans were inferior?

NATIONAL STANDARDS CORRELATIONS:

NCSS Xg: (Civil Ideals & Practices) Analyze the influence of diverse forms of public opinion on the development of public policy and decision-making.
NSH Era 5, Standard 3: How various Reconstruction plans succeeded or failed

WEBSITES:

http://memory.loc.gov/mss/mssmisc/ody/ody0605/0605001v.jpg
"'Atlanta Exposition Speech,' September 18, 1895," The Library of Congress

http://memory.loc.gov/ammem/today/may18.html
"Today in History: May 18," The Library of Congress

http://usinfo.state.gov/usa/infousa/facts/democrac/33.htm
"Introduction to the Court Opinion on the *Plessy v. Ferguson* Case," U.S. Department of State

Founding the NAACP

The first decade of the 20th century was difficult for African-Americans in the North and the South. Lynch mobs formed as easily as thunderclouds and struck as hard as lightning bolts. Race riots became commonplace around the country. In 1904, two African-Americans in Statesboro, Georgia, were accused of murdering a white farmer and his family. Community anger was so high that the militia was called out to protect the jail, but they were not provided with ammunition. The mob stormed the jail where the men were being held and brutally murdered the prisoners. Then it went on a rampage of killing and beating. The mob's leaders were never punished.

W.E.B. DuBois

The 1906 Atlanta race riot began after four women charged that they had been assaulted by African-American men, and again a mob attacked the African-Americans. As a result, this time the African-Americans were armed themselves, and they killed a policeman. Then things got completely out of control, and four African-Americans were killed. White and African-American leaders saw the need for improving race relations and formed the Atlanta Civic League.

To African-Americans like W.E.B. DuBois and William Trotter, this was a clear indication that Booker T. Washington's policies were not working. Born in Massachusetts, DuBois had been educated at Fisk, Harvard, and the University of Berlin. He received his Ph.D. at Harvard in 1895. A noted scholar, he felt that the "talented tenth" among African-Americans were being put down by Washington's program of gradual improvement. William Trotter, also a Harvard graduate, published *The Guardian* to use as "propaganda against discrimination." In 1905, the two men led in the forming of the Niagara Movement. It demanded the vote for African-American men, enforcement of the Constitution, and education for children. It also listed duties: to vote, to work, to obey the law, to be clean and orderly, to send children to school, and to have self-respect.

In 1908, a race riot occurred in Springfield, Illinois—the hometown of Abraham Lincoln. Three whites (William Walling, Mary White Ovington, and Dr. Henry Moskowitz) were shocked and called for a national meeting to discuss "present evils" and to renew the "struggle for civil and political liberty." Their appeal was published by Oscar Garrison Villard, grandson of the famous abolitionist William Lloyd Garrison. They invited members of the Niagara movement to their meeting, and nearly all came. Also there were such notables as Jane Addams, William Dean Howells, and John Dewey.

In 1910, the group formally took the name of National Association for the Advancement of Colored People and chose its officers. All were white except for DuBois, but he was named editor of the NAACP's magazine, *The Crisis.* The Legal Redress committee was set up to take race-related cases to court.

RESULTS: DuBois and other African-Americans had founded a method of protesting not only racial injustice, but the policies of Booker T. Washington. The Legal Redress committee would win many important cases in the years ahead.

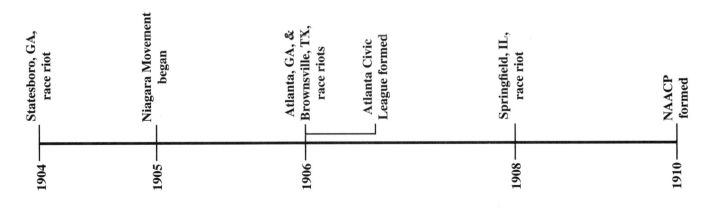

Statesboro, GA, race riot — 1904

Niagara Movement began — 1905

Atlanta, GA, & Brownsville, TX, race riots — 1906

Atlanta Civic League formed

Springfield, IL, race riot — 1908

NAACP formed — 1910

Name: _____   Date: _____

Founding the NAACP: Reinforcement

Directions: Complete the following activities, essays, and challenges on your own paper.

ACTIVITIES:

1. Ask a representative of the NAACP to talk to your class.
2. If your class has a large African-American representation, have students ask their parents' and grandparents' opinions of the NAACP.

ESSAYS:

1. What kinds of conditions do you think it would take for a riot to take place in your hometown?
2. After reviewing the list of demands put on African-Americans by the Niagara Movement, what do you think their purpose was?
3. The original executive committee of the NAACP included only one African-American (DuBois). Why do you think that was?

CHALLENGES:

1. What punishment did the rioters at Statesboro receive?
2. What group formed because of the Atlanta riot?
3. Who was the first African-American to receive a Ph.D. from an American university?
4. Who published *The Guardian?*
5. What group was started by DuBois and Trotter?
6. What were the demands of their movement?
7. What duties did they list for African-Americans?
8. What made the Springfield riot more important than others?
9. What were the last names of the three leaders who called for a national meeting of whites and African-Americans to discuss racial problems?
10. What name was given to the NAACP magazine?

NATIONAL STANDARDS CORRELATIONS:

NCSS Vf: (Individuals, Groups, & Institutions) Describe the role of institutions in furthering both continuity and change.
NSH Era 6, Standard 2: Massive immigration after 1870 and how new social patterns, conflicts, and ideas of national unity developed amid growing cultural diversity

WEBSITES:

http://www.naacp.org
"National Association for the Advancement of Colored People: Making Democracy Work Since 1909," NAACP

http://www.duboislc.org/html/DuBoisBio.html
"Biographical Sketch of W.E.B. DuBois by Gerald Hynes," The W.E.B. DuBois Learning Center

http://www.yale.edu/glc/archive/1152.htm
"Niagara's Declaration of Principles, 1905," The Gilder Lehrman Center for the Study of Slavery, Resistance, & Abolition

The Urban League

For the Southern African-Americans who moved to the northern city, it was as dramatic an experience as coming to America had been for the European. Leaving the way of life one has always had and moving to a different environment required a great adjustment. Finding a place to live, looking for work, filling out applications, traffic, street names, crowded stores, being removed from family and friends, and the criminal element who found them easy marks made it a frightening experience.

NYC in the 1900s

Yet, they kept coming. In a 1908 article, Ray Stannard Baker reported that an "army of Negroes" was gathering not only in the South, but in the West Indies, South Africa, and South America, ready to move to northern cities. Job opportunities were better for women than men, but a few men were starting their own businesses and working their way up in clerical and professional jobs.

In 1905, two committees formed in New York City: one to improve industrial conditions for African-American workers and the other to help African-American women. At the same time, George Haynes, an African-American graduate student at Columbia University, was writing about social and economic conditions of African-Americans in the city. He spoke before a joint meeting of the two groups, and out of that meeting and others that followed, the National Urban League was born in 1911. Its mission was to help African-Americans by researching problems and then devising methods of solving them. Among the areas of focus were housing, health, sanitation, recreation, self-improvement, and job assistance.

Branches opened in most large cities. Migrants were met at the train, directed to housing and jobs, and offered information about living in the city. Another focus was to train African-American social workers to help meet the needs of the new arrivals.

The NAACP and Urban League had neither the resources nor the ability to handle all the problems. Other groups also helped in the adjustment. African-American churches provided educational and social programs. St. Philip's Protestant Episcopal Church in New York bought ten new apartment houses that were intended for white occupants and rented them to African-American tenants. The Young Men's Christian Association (YMCA) and Young Women's Christian Association (YWCA) also provided social, recreational, and educational opportunities.

The YMCA movement received a big boost when Julius Rosenwald and N.W. Harris each pledged $25,000 to build a YMCA—if the African-American community raised $50,000. Within three weeks, African-Americans contributed $65,000. Rosenwald then widened his offer of a $25,000 donation to any African-American community that raised an equal amount. Fraternal orders like the Masons, Odd Fellows, and the Knights of Pythias provided social outlets.

RESULTS: Thanks to the Urban League, YMCA, YWCA, and African-American fraternal orders and churches, the transition was made much easier for African-Americans coming from the South.

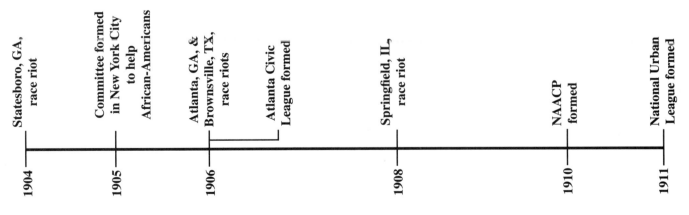

Timeline:
- 1904 — Statesboro, GA, race riot
- 1905 — Committee formed in New York City to help African-Americans
- 1906 — Atlanta, GA, & Brownsville, TX, race riots; Atlanta Civic League formed
- 1908 — Springfield, IL, race riot
- 1910 — NAACP formed
- 1911 — National Urban League formed

Name: _____ Date: _____

The Urban League: Reinforcement

Directions: Complete the following activities, essays, and challenges on your own paper.

ACTIVITIES:

1. Remind students that many Southern African-Americans were illiterate or barely literate, and have the class discuss the problems they faced in the city.
2. Ask what role social agencies play today that private groups had to play in an earlier time. Which system does the class think is the most personal and most effective way to really help people?

ESSAYS:

1. If you had been encouraged to come North by the *Chicago Defender* or some other African-American newspaper, how would you have felt as you got off the train in Chicago?
2. If there had been no Urban League, or no one else to help, what would have happened on your first day in the city?
3. As an African-American who received help from the Urban League and other groups, write about your first day in the city.

CHALLENGES:

1. Besides the America's South, from what countries were African-Americans coming?
2. What part of the African-American urban condition interested George Haynes?
3. When was the Urban League formed?
4. On what areas did the Urban League focus?
5. How did it help the newly arrived migrant?
6. What did St. Philip's Church do to help the housing shortage?
7. What areas were of concern to the YMCA and YWCA?
8. What happened after Rosenwald and Harris pledged $50,000 to help build a YMCA?
9. What promise did Rosenwald make afterward?
10. What fraternal orders were important to African-Americans?

NATIONAL STANDARDS CORRELATIONS:

NCSS Vf: (Individuals, Groups, & Institutions) Describe the role of institutions in furthering both continuity and change.
NSH Era 7, Standard 1: How Progressives and others addressed problems of industrial capitalism, urbanization, and political corruption

WEBSITES:

http://memory.loc.gov/mss/mssmisc/ody/ody0622/0622001v.jpg
"Minutes of the First Meeting of the Committee on Urban Conditions among Negroes Held at the School of Philanthropy, September 29, 1910," The Library of Congress

http://www.dol.gov/asp/programs/history/shfgpr00.htm
"The Federal Government and Negro Workers Under President Woodrow Wilson," U.S. Department of Labor

http://newdeal.feri.org/opp/opp35328.htm
"A Dream, A Quarter Century, A Reality! How the Urban League Has Served, Eugene Kinckle Jones," New Deal Network

African-Americans in World War I

Shoulder patch of 92nd Division

In the presidential election of 1912, African-Americans had no pleasant choices. Taft, in a speech at Howard University, said that the race was peculiarly fit to be farmers. When Theodore Roosevelt's Progressives rejected an NAACP plank against discrimination, African-Americans turned to the Democrats on the basis of Woodrow Wilson's vague statements about justice toward them. Wilson's executive order segregating federal restrooms and eating facilities suggested that the Democrats were a poor alternative.

When World War I broke out in Europe in 1914, military orders and a sudden drop in European immigration caused a surge in employment opportunities in northern factories. Encouraged by African-American newspapers, a new migration of African-Americans headed north. By 1920, 1.5 million African-American jobs were in the North. Those who went found that higher wages were offset by expenses.

When the United States entered the war in 1917, Wilson said America's aim was to "make the world safe for democracy." About 10,000 African-Americans were already in the army, and 15,000 more were in militia units. Those African-Americans trying to enlist after war was declared were often rejected, but when the draft came, they were included. Of the nearly 2.3 million African-Americans registered for the draft, 367,000 ended up in the army. The issue of whether African-Americans would serve under white or African-American officers came up, and Joel Spingarn discussed it with General Leonard Wood. The general told him that if 200 African-Americans of college quality could be found, a training camp for African-American officers would be established. Within ten days, a list of 1,500 college student volunteers was submitted. In October 1917, 630 African-American officers were commissioned in one ceremony.

In 1917, Secretary of War Newton Baker appointed Emmett Scott as his "confidential advisor" in race relations. Until the death of Booker T. Washington in 1915, Scott had served as his personal secretary and was highly regarded by both whites and African-Americans.

An African-American division, the 92nd, was formed; but unlike others, it was trained at seven different camps and did not come together until it was sent to France. The 93rd division was approved but never fully developed; in France, its men were dispersed among French divisions.

Most African-American units going to France worked at arduous, non-combat jobs—unloading ships, labor battalions, etc. The first African-American combat troops to see action were in the 369th Infantry. After receiving further training from the French, these troops were sent to the line where they engaged in 191 days of combat. The Germans called them "Hell Fighters," and the French gave the entire unit the Croix de Guerre (Cross of Honor). Other African-American units also suffered high casualties, including the 370th Infantry, which fought in the last battle of the war.

RESULTS: The experience in France gave African-Americans another chance to prove their loyalty and willingness to fight for the United States. It also gave them the learning experience of being treated as equals for the first time.

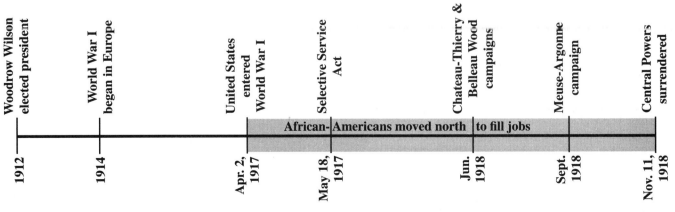

Woodrow Wilson elected president	World War I began in Europe	United States entered World War I	Selective Service Act	Chateau-Thierry & Belleau Wood campaigns	Meuse-Argonne campaign	Central Powers surrendered
1912	1914	Apr. 2, 1917	May 18, 1917	Jun. 1918	Sept. 1918	Nov. 11, 1918

African-Americans moved north to fill jobs

Name: _____ Date: _____

African-Americans in World War I: Reinforcement

Directions: Complete the following activities, essays, and challenges on your own paper.

ACTIVITIES:

1. After reading about World War I, ask the class what life was like at the front for the African-American soldiers who went to France.
2. Discuss the kinds of problems New York militia troops who trained in the South might have (and did have) with southern whites.

ESSAYS:

1. Wilson said America's purpose in entering the war was "to make the world safe for democracy." As an African-American at the time, why would that be (or not be) a good reason for supporting the war effort?
2. What arguments would you have given for putting African-American units under African-American officers?
3. Why did African-American units feel they had to prove something? Do you think they did?

CHALLENGES:

1. Why were African-Americans upset with Wilson?
2. Why did job opportunities open for African-Americans in 1914?
3. How many African-Americans were in the army and militia when the United States entered the war?
4. How many African-Americans entered the army through the draft?
5. Who was the officer who established African-American officer training camps?
6. Who served as "confidential advisor" to the secretary of war? What position had the man previously held?
7. What was unusual about the way the 92nd was trained?
8. What types of jobs did most African-American soldiers perform in France?
9. What African-American unit was called "Hell Fighters" by the Germans?
10. What unit fought in the last battle of the war?

NATIONAL STANDARDS CORRELATIONS:

NCSS IVb: (Individual Development & Identity) Describe personal connections to place—as associated with community, nation, and world.
NSH Era 7, Standard 2: The changing role of the United States in world affairs through World War I

WEBSITES:

http://memory.loc.gov/ammem/aaohtml/exhibit/aopart7.html
"World War I and Postwar Society," The Library of Congress

http://www.lib.byu.edu/~rdh/wwi/comment/Scott/ScottTC.htm#
"Scott's Official History of the American Negro in the World War," Brigham Young University Library

http://www.archives.gov/education/lessons/369th-infantry/
"Teaching With Documents: Photographs of the 369th Infantry and African-Americans during World War I," The U.S. National Archives and Records Administration

Postwar America

The African-Americans returning from the war "to make the world safe for democracy" found a nation that was unsafe for themselves and for others who challenged the status quo. Immigrants with socialist political views were silenced or chased out of the country during the Red Scare. Many with German or Jewish names found it easier to succeed if they dropped their ethnic name for one that was more American. African-American soldiers who returned expecting that their wearing of an army uniform had changed their status were disappointed. African-Americans who had jobs in factories found more hostility as white soldiers returned from the army and expected their old jobs back.

Segregated water fountain

In the long, hot summer of 1919, racial tension grew, and 25 riots occurred. The most important of these was in Chicago, where an incident on the Lake Michigan waterfront led to 13 days of chaos and the deaths of 25 African-Americans and 15 whites. Other riots were at Omaha, Nebraska; Tulsa, Oklahoma; Knoxville, Tennessee; and Elaine, Arkansas. A group of white southerners, led by Will Alexander, joined with African-American leaders in forming the Commission on Interracial Cooperation in 1919. Their efforts did not reach far enough to help most African-Americans; however, the existence of such a group was significant.

A sinister threat was developing. The Ku Klux Klan, dormant since Reconstruction, was given new respectability by the first full-length movie, *Birth of a Nation,* which glorified its role in saving the South from carpetbaggers and African-American rule. Reorganized in 1915 by William Simmons, it grew very slowly until 1920, when two professional fundraisers took over and began a highly successful membership drive. The Imperial Wizard and other top officials made money off memberships and items they sold: horse robes (required whether the Klansman owned a horse or not) sold for $6.50, and a bottle of the water that was required for initiations cost $10. The Klan had at least two million members by 1925 and was strong not only in the South, but in Indiana, Oregon, and other northern states as well.

The new Klan attacked not only African-Americans, but also Catholics, Jews, immigrants, and prohibition violators. It was powerful in both parties, and many in politics knew that opposing it was dangerous to a political future. It was strong enough to get an anti-Klan governor of Oklahoma impeached, and to deny Al Smith the Democratic nomination in 1924. Its decline was rapid after the head of the Klan in Indiana, David Stephenson, was found guilty of causing the death of a secretary.

Even if the new Klan's power was short-lived, and even though many members joined out of a desire to belong somewhere, it was no less brutal and dangerous than it had been the first time around.

RESULTS: African-Americans who hoped that the worst times were all behind them felt new pressures, even in the North. Riots in cities, Klan rallies in small towns and rural areas, and continued economic hard times made some African-Americans think about returning to Africa.

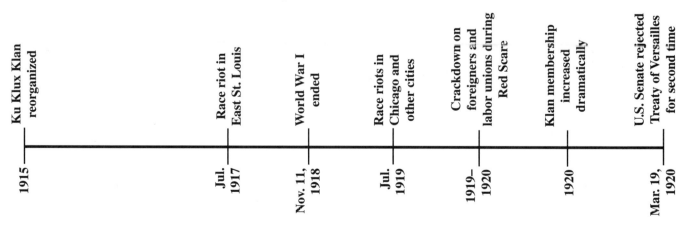

Ku Klux Klan reorganized	Race riot in East St. Louis	World War I ended	Race riots in Chicago and other cities	Crackdown on foreigners and labor unions during Red Scare	Klan membership increased dramatically	U.S. Senate rejected Treaty of Versailles for second time
1915	Jul. 1917	Nov. 11, 1918	Jul. 1919	1919–1920	1920	Mar. 19, 1920

Name: _____ Date: _____

Postwar America: Reinforcement

Directions: Complete the following activities, essays, and challenges on your own paper.

ACTIVITIES:

1. Using a recent riot as an example, what kinds of things happen, and who suffers the most?
2. Ask your students to list the kinds of radical groups of today that resemble the Ku Klux Klan of the 1920s.

ESSAYS:

1. Do you think it can be expected that when there is a riot in one city, there will be riots in others as well? Why or why not?
2. What reasons do you think might have been given by people joining the Klan in the 1920s?
3. Do you think it was better or worse for African-Americans that the Klan picked on other groups as well? Why or why not?

CHALLENGES:

1. What group suffered the most because of the Red Scare?
2. How many riots occurred in 1919?
3. How long did the Chicago race riot of 1919 last, and how many total people were killed?
4. Which Nebraska city had a riot?
5. What group was formed to ease tension in the South?
6. What movie glorified the Klan?
7. Who reorganized the Klan?
8. Name two northern states that had large Klans.
9. Who, besides African-Americans, were targets of the Klan?
10. What presidential hopeful lost the nomination because of Klan opposition?

NATIONAL STANDARDS CORRELATIONS:

NCSS IVb: (Individual Development & Identity) Describe personal connections to place—as associated with community, nation, and world.
NSH Era 7, Standard 3: How the United States changed from the end of World War I to the eve of the Great Depression

WEBSITES:

http://diaspora.northwestern.edu/mbin/WebObjects/DiasporaX.woa/wa/displayArticle?atomid=602
"Chicago Race Riot of 1919," The Institute for Diasporic Studies, Northwestern University

http://historymatters.gmu.edu/d/4974
"'Says Lax Conditions Caused Race Riots': *Chicago Daily News* and Carl Sandburg Report on the Chicago Race Riot of 1919," American Social History Productions

http://www.digitalhistory.uh.edu/database/article_display.cfm?HHID=443
"The Great Migration," Digital History

Marcus Garvey and Racial Pride

Marcus Garvey

In 1923, a heavy-set African-American man stood in federal court, charged with fraud. His name was Marcus Garvey, and he was often ridiculed and criticized by both whites and African-Americans alike. Yet he appealed to thousands of African-Americans because he offered them things lacking in their lives: hope and pride. Whether he was a Moses, a deluded visionary, or a con man taking advantage of uneducated African-Americans is still debated.

Born and educated in Jamaica, he was a young man when he discovered he could move crowds with his oratory. He began to demand more rights for the blacks of Jamaica, who stood at the foot of every ladder. After three years of study at London University, he traveled in Europe and North Africa, and then he returned to his homeland to form the Jamaica Improvement Association. He wrote to Booker T. Washington and expressed his interest in starting trade schools in Jamaica based on the Tuskegee model. Washington invited him to come to the United States. By the time he arrived in the United States in 1916, B. T. Washington was dead, and the African-American community had no widely accepted leaders. It also had no interest in its African origins.

Garvey was a dreamer who spoke of the beauties of Africa while standing hungry and cold on a soapbox on a New York street corner. His approach to the race problem was different from others. In a 1923 article, he wrote: "Let the white race stop thinking that all African-American men are dogs ... Let foolish Negro agitators ... stop preaching and advocating the doctrine of 'social equality'..." His solution was for African-Americans to return to the African homeland (either literally or symbolically). His method of creating that homeland was through his organization, the United Negro Improvement Association (UNIA), which eventually grew to at least 500,000 members.

The UNIA intended to make African-Americans independent of whites in all things. It ran its own grocery stores, had Black Cross nurses, and started its own steamship company, the Black Star Line. He designed a red, green, and black flag. UNIA parades were colorful and long, with groups marching with heads held high. In a Madison Square Garden convention, they filled the huge building, with thousands of others outside. He told African-Americans to have pride in what they were and to stop trying to look like whites by straightening their hair and bleaching their skins.

DuBois and the NAACP saw him as a fraud, misleading African-Americans and undercutting their work of bringing social equality to the United States. The most bitter attacks on Garvey were by other African-Americans. When Garvey got into trouble for mail fraud in the sale of Black Star stock, his enemies cheered. After serving two years in prison, he was deported to Jamaica. He died in London in 1940.

RESULTS: Garvey was no businessman, and it was his downfall. His vision of "black pride" became significant in the 1960s. The question of whether African-Americans should develop separately or join the mainstream remained.

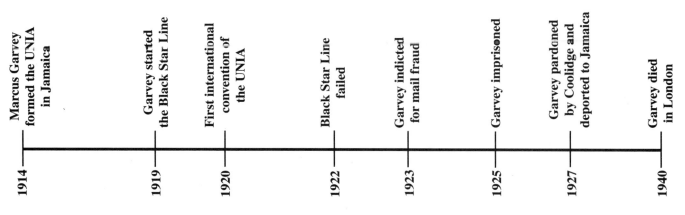

1914	1919	1920	1922	1923	1925	1927	1940
Marcus Garvey formed the UNIA in Jamaica	Garvey started the Black Star Line	First international convention of the UNIA	Black Star Line failed	Garvey indicted for mail fraud	Garvey imprisoned	Garvey pardoned by Coolidge and deported to Jamaica	Garvey died in London

Name: _____ Date: _____

Marcus Garvey and Racial Pride: Reinforcement

Directions: Complete the following activities, essays, and challenges on your own paper.

ACTIVITIES:

1. Ask the class to discuss whether they feel Garvey was right or wrong in his emphasis on Africa and his opposition to working for social equality.
2. Look at the flags of nations. How many can the class find that use the colors green, black, and red?

ESSAYS:

1. Why did most African-American leaders feel that Garvey was hurting their cause?
2. If you were assigned to "build black pride," would you approach it in the same way Garvey did?
3. How would you judge the success or failure of a group like the UNIA?

CHALLENGES:

1. What group did Garvey form in Jamaica?
2. What African-American did he admire?
3. How did Garvey feel about the NAACP's efforts to achieve social equality?
4. What did the initials UNIA stand for?
5. What steamship company did Garvey start?
6. What three colors were on his flag?
7. What were African-Americans doing with their hair and skin that annoyed Garvey?
8. Who was an African-American critic of Garvey?
9. What charge was brought against Garvey in court?
10. What punishment did he receive?

NATIONAL STANDARDS CORRELATIONS:

NCSS Xf: (Civic Ideals & Practices) Identify and explain the roles of formal and informal political actors in influencing and shaping public policy and decision-making.
NSH Era 7, Standard 1: How Progressives and others addressed problems of industrial capitalism, urbanization, and political corruption

WEBSITES:

http://www.pbs.org/wgbh/amex/garvey/
"Marcus Garvey: Look for Me in the Whirlwind," Public Broadcasting Service

http://www.isop.ucla.edu/africa/mgpp/
"The Marcus Garvey and Universal Negro Improvement Association Papers Project," University of California

http://www.nhc.rtp.nc.us:8080/tserve/twenty/tkeyinfo/garvey.htm
"Marcus Garvey and the Universal Negro Improvement Association," National Humanities Center

http://www.unia-acl.org/
"Welcome to the Official UNIA-ACL Website," UNIA-ACL

Ragtime, Jazz, and Blues

Louis Armstrong

The names of very few African-Americans were known or appreciated by most whites during the first two decades of the century. African-American baseball players were limited to the rag-tag teams of the Negro League. The name of Jack Johnson was known among boxing fans, but his behavior outside the ring was unacceptable to most African-Americans and whites. One group of African-Americans, though, was receiving much favorable attention, and white customers lined up to attend its performances in New York, New Orleans, Memphis, and St. Louis. On the stage were African-American musicians, sometimes creating new songs as they played. There were more than songs being born; these were new expressions of the people.

This was not the first time African-Americans created music that whites borrowed and took to heart. The spiritual had been the first—the melancholy prayer of the slave begging God to "let my people go." Then they had made up work songs as they labored in the fields, laid railroad tracks, or dug ditches. After the Civil War, military band instruments were in plentiful supply and could be bought for the price of a little labor or cash. There were also make-shift instruments, and musicians strummed on homemade guitars and banjos, played old pianos, blew horns, and beat on drums. The music came not from a book, but from the heart. The main motive was pleasure rather than financial reward or fame, but some managed to find all three.

Ragtime became popular around 1900. It was highly syncopated music, usually played on the piano; the left hand played the rhythm, and the right hand played a bright and cheerful melody. The best-known ragtime writer was Scott Joplin, whose fame came from such songs as "The Entertainer" and "Maple Leaf Rag."

It is said that the blues grew out of the songs of the slaves and has a sorrowful sound and message. W.C. Handy wore the title of "Father of the Blues," and two of the most famous blues songs were written by him: "Memphis Blues" and "St. Louis Blues." The message of the blues is in both the words and the melody: "I feel like running, running way away, Ain't got nobody, and nowhere to stay." The best-known blues vocalist was Billie Holliday.

Jazz was born in New Orleans, with both African and European music as its parents. The first jazz band director was Joe "King" Oliver, who took a basic melody and improvised from it. Duke Ellington's and Count Basie's reputations have long since surpassed Oliver's. Their bands drew international attention.

RESULTS: It was through music that slaves expressed themselves, and music was an important way for African-Americans to again express their feelings, and in such a way that others would be influenced by their message.

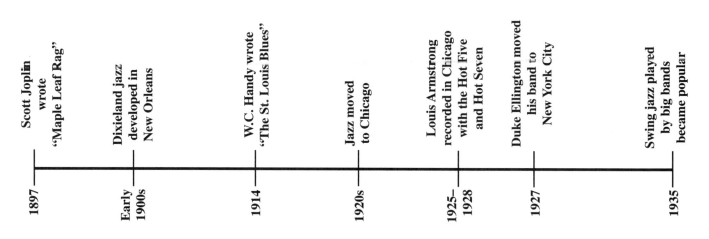

Scott Joplin wrote "Maple Leaf Rag" — 1897

Dixieland jazz developed in New Orleans — Early 1900s

W.C. Handy wrote "The St. Louis Blues" — 1914

Jazz moved to Chicago — 1920s

Louis Armstrong recorded in Chicago with the Hot Five and Hot Seven — 1925–1928

Duke Ellington moved his band to New York City — 1927

Swing jazz played by big bands became popular — 1935

Name: _____ Date: _____

Ragtime, Jazz, and Blues: Reinforcement

Directions: Complete the following activities, essays, and challenges on your own paper.

ACTIVITIES:

1. Listen to some spirituals and then to blues, and see if the class finds any similarities or differences between them.
2. Make a list of famous African-American musicians and the style of music they have written or performed.

ESSAYS:

1. How does a person express his or her feelings through music? If you are happy, sad, angry, or lonely, to what type of music do you choose to listen?
2. After listening to some blues, ragtime, or jazz, how do you think it compares to more contemporary music?
3. After reading about an early African-American performer, discuss what kinds of problems African-American performers faced in becoming successful.

CHALLENGES:

1. What were four centers for African-American musicians?
2. What were two earlier music forms created by African-Americans?
3. Where did African-American musicians find instruments they could afford?
4. What was the main motive of these post-Civil War musicians?
5. What instrument was usually used for ragtime?
6. Who was the most important ragtime composer and musician?
7. What were two of the most famous ragtime songs?
8. Who was the "Father of the Blues"?
9. What were two of the most famous blues songs?
10. Who were two of the most famous jazz band directors?

NATIONAL STANDARDS CORRELATIONS:

NCSS Ic: (Culture) Explain and give examples of how language, literature, the arts, architecture, other artifacts, traditions, beliefs, values, and behaviors contribute to the development and transmission of culture.

NSH Era 7, Standard 3: How the United States changed from the end of World War I to the eve of the Great Depression

WEBSITES:

http://128.143.22.16/harlem/contents.html
"The Survey Graphic Harlem Number," University of Virginia

http://www.scottjoplin.org/biography.htm
"A Biography of Scott Joplin: (c.1867–1917)," The Scott Joplin International Ragtime Foundation

http://memory.loc.gov/ammem/award97/rpbhtml/aasmhome.html
"African-American Sheet Music 1850–1920," The Library of Congress

The New Deal

Most African-Americans had been Republicans since the Civil War, and the party had returned the favor with jobs and influence. But African-American loyalty to the party was rarely returned in equal portion. Republicans may have neglected African-Americans, but at least the Republicans were not hostile to them, which was more than could be said for southern Democrats. In 1928, Oscar DePriest, a Chicago Republican, was elected to the House—the first African-American in Congress in the twentieth century. DePriest was more than just the Representative of the First Illinois District; he was the spokesman for every African-American in the nation. African-Americans long alienated from politics began to take an interest in it again. African-American influence helped defeat the nomination of John Parker to the Supreme Court, then turned on Parker's Senate supporters, helping to defeat some of them.

CCC Worker

The beginning of an African-American switching of allegiance came during the 1928 campaign. Hoover's success in breaking the Solid South caused many Republican leaders to see a potential new market for the party; they would gladly trade off the African-American vote for the South's electoral vote. The walk away from the Republican party was to become a stampede after the Depression came. Even DePriest felt the impact, and he lost the 1934 election to Arthur Mitchell, the first African-American Democrat in Congressional history.

Franklin D. Roosevelt's New Deal affected African-Americans in many ways. One was the willingness of some New Dealers to work with African-Americans. Harold Ickes, an active NAACP leader, was secretary of the interior, and he appointed African-American advisors. Dr. Will Alexander headed the Farm Security Administration (FSA), and his agency helped many African-American farmers. Roosevelt often met with African-American leaders in the "Black Cabinet" or the "Black Brain Trust." Mrs. Roosevelt had less to fear from southern Democrats than her husband and made herself the target for their wrath when she became friendly with Mrs. Mary McLeod Bethune, an African-American activist and member of the National Youth Administration. Mrs. Roosevelt visited African-American schools and was photographed being escorted by two members of the Howard University's Reserve Officers' Training Corps (ROTC).

New Deal agencies had a mixed record when it came to African-Americans. The National Recovery Act (NRA) wrote codes of fair competition in industry, and many codes allowed African-American workers to receive lower wages than whites. The Agricultural Adjustment Act (AAA) paid farmers to take land out of production; many southern landowners signed AAA agreements and kicked tenant farmers and sharecroppers off the land. The Civilian Conservation Corps (CCC) employed many young African-American males in its conservation projects, but they were always in segregated camps. The Public Works Administration (PWA) and the Works Progress Administration (WPA) work projects included thousands of African-American workers, and they improved facilities on African-American college campuses, playgrounds, and community centers.

RESULTS: The New Deal did not solve all the economic and social problems of African-Americans, but it did provide jobs and relief to many who were desperately in need of help. Roosevelt was never more popular with any group than he was with the nation's African-Americans, as their switch in parties indicated.

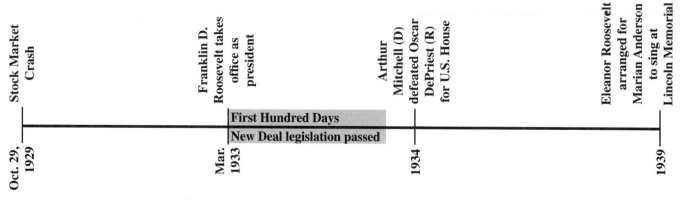

Stock Market Crash	Franklin D. Roosevelt takes office as president	Arthur Mitchell (D) defeated Oscar DePriest (R) for U.S. House	Eleanor Roosevelt arranged for Marian Anderson to sing at Lincoln Memorial
	First Hundred Days		
	New Deal legislation passed		
Oct. 29, 1929	Mar. 1933	1934	1939

Name: _____ Date: _____

The New Deal: Reinforcement

Directions: Complete the following activities, essays, and challenges on your own paper.

ACTIVITIES:

1. DePriest represented African-Americans from all across the nation. Ask the class if they feel that African-American representatives in Congress or the state legislature today play that same role.
2. Ask the class if they think it was a good idea for the vast majority of African-Americans to switch to the Democrats.

ESSAYS:

1. Even though Eleanor Roosevelt held no government job, why was she important to African-Americans in the 1930s?
2. As an African-American who switched parties in the 1930s, explain why you became a Democrat.
3. As an African-American Republican in the 1930s, explain why you did not switch parties.

CHALLENGES:

1. What distinction did Oscar DePriest have?
2. What Supreme Court nominee was defeated partly because of African-American opposition?
3. Why did Hoover's victory in 1928 hurt Republican relations with African-Americans?
4. What ended DePriest's career in Congress?
5. What prominent NAACP official was an important New Dealer?
6. What nickname was given to Roosevelt's African-American advisors?
7. What agency was important to African-Americans looking for industrial jobs?
8. What program resulted in sharecroppers losing land?
9. What agency used young African-American men in conservation projects?
10. What did the Works Progress Administration (WPA) and the Public Works Administration (PWA) do that had an impact on African-Americans?

NATIONAL STANDARDS CORRELATIONS:

NCSS Xj: (Civic Ideals & Practices) Examine strategies designed to strengthen the "common good," which consider a range of options for citizen action.
NSH Era 8, Standard 2: How the New Deal addressed the Great Depression, transformed American federalism, and initiated the welfare state

WEBSITES:

http://memory.loc.gov/ammem/aaohtml/exhibit/aopart8.html
"The Depression, The New Deal, and World War II," The Library of Congress

http://www.pbs.org/wgbh/amex/dustbowl/peopleevents/pandeAMEX05.html
"The Great Depression," Public Broadcasting Service

http://www.loc.gov/exhibits/african/afam012.html
"The African-American Mosaic: WPA," The Library of Congress

http://newdeal.feri.org/aaccc/
"African-Americans in the Civilian Conservation Corps," New Deal Network

Jobs Created by World War II

In 1939, war again broke out in Europe, and factories that had been long closed by the Depression reopened. African-American workers, tired of being unemployed or working on New Deal projects at low wages, were anxious to get a "real" job with higher wages.

Some industrial jobs had been open to African-Americans for many years, and others opened in the 1930s. The United Mine Workers (UMW) had always encouraged African-American membership. When UMW president John L. Lewis formed the Congress of Industrial Organizations (CIO) in 1935, the CIO recruited African-Americans from the beginning. The longshoreman's union (IL&WU) brought African-American workers into their dock gangs, and the United Auto Workers (UAW) helped African-Americans get better jobs in auto plants. CIO efforts in employment removed many African-Americans' suspicions of unions.

worker in Norfolk Navy Yard

African-American awareness of the growing world threat increased in the 1930s, especially when Italy attacked the African nation of Ethiopia and when Hitler's racism became better known. At the 1936 Berlin Olympics, Hitler refused to present Jesse Owens with the four medals he had earned. Max Schmeling's knockout of Joe Louis in 1936 added to the African-Americans' anger with the Germans. However, it did sweeten the revenge when Louis defeated Schmeling in 1938. However, the Aryan superiority and expansionist policies of Hitler were far more serious than his bad sportsmanship, and African-Americans supported Roosevelt's efforts to build American military preparedness.

The long-standing practice of refusing to hire African-Americans continued in many industries, even though there were shortages of available workers. At first, the government tried gentle pressure on businesses with defense contracts through the National Defense Advisory Committee and the Office of Production Management (OPM). Their efforts failed to accomplish much; that was when A. Philip Randolph stepped in.

Randolph had organized the Brotherhood of Sleeping Car Porters in 1925 and became an American Federation of Labor (AFL) vice president. Irritated by the slow progress in employing African-Americans, Randolph proposed that African-Americans stage a march on Washington on July 1, 1941. Many people, both African-American and white, tried to change Randolph's mind, and finally Roosevelt proposed a compromise. If Randolph called off the march, the president would issue an order prohibiting discrimination in government and in defense industries. Randolph finally agreed, and Roosevelt issued Executive Order 8802. It required that there be no discrimination in employment of workers in defense plants "because of race, creed, color, or national origin." A Committee on Fair Employment Practices was set up to investigate complaints.

RESULTS: Even though it had no power to deny a defense contract to a company, the investigations and hearings of the Committee on Fair Employment Practices were enough to change the policies of some, and thousands of African-Americans found new job opportunities.

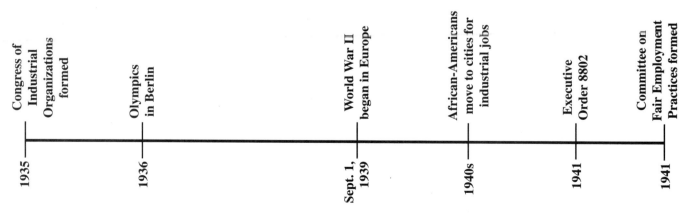

1935	1936	Sept. 1, 1939	1940s	1941	1941
Congress of Industrial Organizations formed	Olympics in Berlin	World War II began in Europe	African-Americans move to cities for industrial jobs	Executive Order 8802	Committee on Fair Employment Practices formed

Name: _____ Date: _____

Jobs Created by World War II: Reinforcement

Directions: Complete the following activities, essays, and challenges on your own paper.

ACTIVITIES:

1. A labor union today is slow to accept African-American members. Ask the class to prepare a list of reasons, other than legal, why it is in their best interests to accept African-Americans.
2. Ask the class what kinds of groups are protected by "race, creed, color, or national origin."

ESSAYS:

1. Do you think a march on Washington was a good idea? What kinds of reasons would you have given Randolph to do it or not to do it?
2. Why do you think that the treatment of Jesse Owens and the knockout of Joe Louis caused African-Americans to feel despondent in the late 1930s? What type of situation might cause African-Americans to feel the same way today?
3. Why did so few unions show an interest in recruiting African-Americans? What kinds of reasons do you think they gave?

CHALLENGES:

1. What major union had always been open to African-Americans?
2. What attitude did the Congress of Industrial Organizations take toward African-Americans?
3. What Olympic medalist was not honored by Hitler?
4. Who boxed twice against Joe Louis?
5. What were the initials of the two agencies trying to persuade businesses to hire African-Americans?
6. What American Federation of Labor union was organized by A. Philip Randolph?
7. What was Randolph's part of the compromise with Roosevelt?
8. What was Roosevelt's part of the compromise?
9. What was the purpose of Executive Order 8802?
10. What committee was set up to investigate complaints?

NATIONAL STANDARDS CORRELATIONS:

NCSS Xj: (Civic Ideals & Practices) Examine strategies designed to strengthen the "common good," which consider a range of options for citizen action.
NSH Era 8, Standard 3: The causes and course of World War II, the character of the war at home and abroad, and its reshaping of the U.S. role in world affairs

WEBSITES:

http://memory.loc.gov/ammem/aaohtml/exhibit/aopart8.html
"The Depression, The New Deal, and World War II," The Library of Congress

http://www.ourdocuments.gov/doc.php?flash=false&doc=72
"Executive Order 8802: Prohibition of Discrimination in the Defense Industry (1941)," The U.S. National Archives and Records Administration

http://www.dol.gov/asp/programs/history/chapter5.htm
"Chapter 5: Americans in Depression and War," U.S. Department of Labor

African-Americans Fight in World War II

As Japanese armies fanned out over Asia and German forces spread across Europe and North Africa, U.S. military strength was noteworthy because of its weakness. In 1939, the army had 334,000 men, with the 5,000 African-Americans still limited to the historic 9th and 10th Cavalries and 24th and 25th Infantries. When Selective Service began in 1940, draft boards often passed over African-Americans; the law was amended, and draft boards were ordered to stop discriminating.

It was clear that the army had no intention of mixing races, so leaders could only demand that (1) African-Americans should be trained by the African-American reserve officers available, (2) medical teams be integrated, and (3) African-Americans be appointed to draft boards and as assistants in the War and Navy departments. Reserve Officers' Training

WWII African-American soldiers

Corps (ROTC) units were created at some African-American colleges, and Colonel B.O. Davis was promoted to brigadier general—the first African-American general in American history.

About one million African-Americans served in the armed forces in World War II, half of whom were sent overseas. Army units were segregated as in World War I, and most African-Americans served under white officers. About 4,000 African-American women served in the Womens' Auxiliary Corps (WACs). African-American pilots were trained for the Air Force at Tuskegee, Alabama, and their ground crews were trained at Chanute Field, Illinois.

The navy had only used African-Americans as cooks and servants. In 1942, the navy allowed African-Americans to be enlisted, and a separate camp to train African-American sailors was established at the Great Lakes Training Center. African-American women were accepted into the Women's Reserve of the Navy, or Women Accepted for Volunteer Emergency Service (WAVES). Marines did not accept African-Americans until later in the war. After admitting a few African-Americans, the corps pronounced the experiment a success.

By the end of the war, almost 500,000 African-Americans were serving in the European theater: unloading ships, driving trucks, building camps, and delivering ordnance. Many were in the thick of battle; the 761st Tank Battalion was in the Battle of the Bulge, and the 614th Tank Destroyer Battalion was in combat many times. Other units were in Asia, building the Ledo Road, or fighting their way through the Japanese-held islands.

It was a difficult battle for freedom when segregation constantly confronted the African-American soldier. Jackie Robinson, a young lieutenant, refused to move to the back of a bus and faced a court martial for the incident. Some African-American soldiers were refused entrance to a Kansas cafe, but they saw German prisoners of war (POWs) being served inside. As soldiers heard of the race riot in Detroit, African-American soldiers must have wondered what lay ahead for them after the war.

RESULTS: Again, African-American soldiers proved their mettle in combat, and they did much of the hard work behind the scenes that made victories possible.

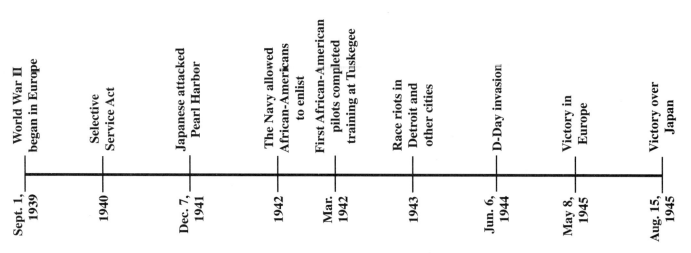

World War II began in Europe	Selective Service Act	Japanese attacked Pearl Harbor	The Navy allowed African-Americans to enlist	First African-American pilots completed training at Tuskegee	Race riots in Detroit and other cities	D-Day invasion	Victory in Europe	Victory over Japan
Sept. 1, 1939	1940	Dec. 7, 1941	1942	Mar. 1942	1943	Jun. 6, 1944	May 8, 1945	Aug. 15, 1945

Name: _____ Date: _____

African-Americans Fight in World War II: Reinforcement

Directions: Complete the following activities, essays, and challenges on your own paper.

ACTIVITIES:

1. Have the class make a list of reasons African-Americans might have had for supporting the war and the reasons they might have given for wanting to stay out of it.
2. Discuss ways in which the class thinks that the war might have affected the civil rights movement that grew afterward.

ESSAYS:

1. In what kinds of ways did African-Americans serve their country in the U.S. military?
2. What motives do you think African-Americans had for wanting to serve in World War II?
3. As an African-American soldier in 1945, write a letter home telling your parents what you think postwar America should be like.

CHALLENGES:

1. How many African-American soldiers were there in 1939?
2. After Selective Service began, how did most draft boards deal with African-Americans?
3. Who was the first African-American general in American history?
4. How many African-Americans went overseas?
5. How many African-American WACs were there in the army?
6. Where were African-American pilots trained?
7. What was the result of the "experiment" with African-American marines?
8. Name two African-American units in the European War.
9. Why did the incident at the Kansas restaurant especially anger African-Americans?
10. Where did a major race riot occur during the war?

NATIONAL STANDARDS CORRELATIONS:

NCSS IVb: (Individual Development & Identity) Describe personal connections to place—as associated with community, nation, and world.
NSH Era 8, Standard 3: The causes and course of World War II, the character of the war at home and abroad, and its reshaping of the U.S. role in world affairs

WEBSITES:

http://memory.loc.gov/ammem/aaohtml/exhibit/aopart8.html
"The Depression, The New Deal, and World War II," The Library of Congress

http://www.wpafb.af.mil/museum/history/prewwii/ta.html
"Tuskegee Airmen," National Museum of the United States Air Force

http://www.loc.gov/exhibits/treasures/trm116.html
"The 332nd Fighter Group," The Library of Congress

http://www.army.mil/cmh-pg/books/wwii/11-4/
"United States Army in World War II, Special Studies, The Employment of Negro Troops by Ulysses Lee," U.S. Army Center of Military History

Truman Stands Up for Equality

It was clear to most observers that race relations during the war had been less than perfect. Anyone who doubted had only to read Gunnar Myrdal's book, *An American Dilemma* (1944). He saw the race problem as one not only between groups, but within individuals, and even the most prejudiced person still housed the "American creed of liberty, equality, justice, and fair opportunity for everybody." To paraphrase Lincoln, Americans just needed to "release the better angels of their nature."

1948 Democratic Convention

The death of Roosevelt in April 1945 gave African-Americans reasons to be concerned. His successor, Harry Truman, was an unknown quantity. Born and raised in a border state, Truman had been a loyal supporter of New Deal programs; but whether that meant he supported the ideals of racial equality remained to be seen. Their only clue as to the policies he might follow was that he had clashed loudly with the KKK during the 1920s, when it had tried to keep him from hiring Irish army veterans for public works in Jackson County, Missouri.

In 1946, Truman appointed a Civil Rights Commission to study the condition of African-Americans. With representatives from both races agreeing to its conclusions, the Commission reported that civil rights were being denied to minority citizens. It recommended that segregation be eliminated. Another commission, reporting on colleges, recommended that discrimination be eliminated in higher education. In 1948, a third commission recommended an end to segregation in the armed forces.

Considering the political dangers of antagonizing the powerful southern Democrats who controlled Congress, Truman had run a risk in even appointing the commissions. To support their reports was even more dangerous, since these men were conservatives who disliked the liberal policies of Roosevelt and Truman in general. When the 1948 Democratic convention was held, a civil rights plank was adopted, and most southern delegates walked out. They formed the Southern Democratic party (Dixiecrats) and ran Senator Strom Thurmond (South Carolina) for president. Truman never gave in to their pressure and actively sought the African-American vote in the North. Truman's reelection surprised many, but the turnout of African-American voters in key northern states was an unexpected ingredient in his success.

Congress was still in the hands of southern Democrats, but Truman moved in areas outside their control. The armed services began to order that jobs be filled by the best qualified personnel, regardless of race. During the Korean War, General Matthew Ridgeway received permission to begin integrating his field units. Truman ordered fair employment of federal civilian personnel without discrimination based on race.

RESULTS: The Civil Rights Commission was a first step in recognizing a problem nearly everyone knew existed. Rather than being content to just study and do nothing, Truman began to change policies despite the risks.

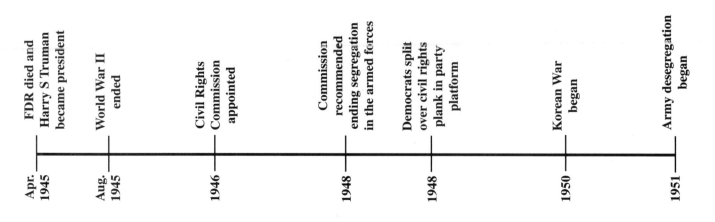

FDR died and Harry S Truman became president — Apr. 1945

World War II ended — Aug. 1945

Civil Rights Commission appointed — 1946

Commission recommended ending segregation in the armed forces — 1948

Democrats split over civil rights plank in party platform — 1948

Korean War began — 1950

Army desegregation began — 1951

Name: _____ Date: _____

Truman Stands Up for Equality: Reinforcement

Directions: Complete the following activities, essays, and challenges on your own paper.

ACTIVITIES:

1. Gunnar Myrdal was Swedish. Ask the class why they think the opinion of an outsider was considered so important in the discussion of race issues.
2. After looking at Truman's record, ask the class how they would have rated his civil rights record against Roosevelt's.

ESSAYS:

1. Some accused Truman of playing politics with race. What did he have to gain and to lose when he campaigned in Harlem in 1948?
2. Presidents have often appointed commissions to study problems. What difference does it make who serves on the commission?
3. Why do you think a president like Truman might achieve less than he wants to accomplish?

CHALLENGES:

1. Who wrote *An American Dilemma?*
2. Why did Myrdal think that American attitudes might change?
3. What was the only basis for hope that African-Americans had when Truman became president?
4. What did the Civil Rights Commission recommend?
5. What did the other commissions recommend?
6. What group was especially angry over the appointments of these commissions?
7. What happened after the civil rights plank was adopted at the Democratic Convention in 1948?
8. By what name was a Southern Democrat usually known in 1948?
9. What general wanted to integrate forces in the field during the Korean War?
10. What change did Truman make in federal employment?

NATIONAL STANDARDS CORRELATIONS:

NCSS Xa: (Civic Ideals & Practices) Examine the origins and continuing influence of key ideals of the democratic republican form of government, such as individual human dignity, liberty, justice, equality, and the rule of law.
NSH Era 9, Standard 3: Domestic policies after World War II

WEBSITES:

http://www.trumanlibrary.org/whistlestop/study_collections/desegregation/large/index.php?action=chronology
"Desegregation of the Armed Forces," Truman Presidential Museum & Library

http:www.ourdocuments.gov/doc.php?flash=false&doc=84
"Executive Order 9981: Desegregation of the Armed Forces (1949)," The U.S. National Archives and Records Administration

http://usinfo.state.gov/usa/infousa/facts/democrac/35.htm
"Harry S Truman," U.S. Department of State

The Landmark *Brown* Decision

NAACP lawyers celebrate victory

Segregation and discrimination were a fact of life for African-Americans in 21 states and the District of Columbia. The Supreme Court's acceptance of segregation in rail transportation in 1896 had given an excuse to discriminate against African-Americans in most other areas of life as well. Cities had tried to pass ordinances designating certain blocks as white and others as African-American, but the Court said "no" to that in 1917. Neighbors signed agreements (restrictive covenants) not to sell their houses to African-Americans; that was also ruled unconstitutional in 1948. Discrimination against African-Americans in court was frequent, but in some cases that went to the Supreme Court, it overturned the guilty verdict because due process had been denied. African-Americans were never called to sit on juries in that county, defendants were given inadequate legal representation, witnesses were whipped to get them to give testimony against the defendant, or the jury was intimidated by a mob inside the courtroom.

The need for African-American lawyers to defend the accused was apparent, but they were rare because southern law schools did not admit African-Americans, and few had the funds or education to go north to law school. The NAACP could not afford to hire enough lawyers to defend all African-Americans accused, but it did have staff lawyers to handle some cases. One was Thurgood Marshall, who traveled through the South, using his old car as an office, and with his old typewriter handy to write appeals.

As long as African-Americans were given an unequal education, the race could never catch up with whites, so one of the main interests of the NAACP was to end segregation in schools. They started by taking cases to court involving higher education (colleges and universities). Their first emphasis was on winning cases involving the training of lawyers. Missouri's practice of sending African-American students out of state to receive law school education was rejected by the Court in 1938. After Texas created a law school admitting African-American students only, the Court ruled in 1950 that the new school was not equal to the University of Texas, and its students must be admitted to the University of Texas. The University of Oklahoma's policy of segregating an African-American student in the classroom, library, and dining hall was also rejected.

In 1954, the Court handed down its 9–0 decision in *Brown v. Board of Education of Topeka,* in which it said that "in the field of public education the doctrine of 'separate but equal' has no place. Separate educational facilities are inherently unequal." The next year, the Court told the states to desegregate "with all deliberate speed." The Plessy mistake had been corrected.

RESULTS: If the Supreme Court or others who cheered the *Brown* decision assumed this was the end of the issue, they were badly mistaken. Strong opposition quickly developed in the Deep South, but along the border, states began to comply.

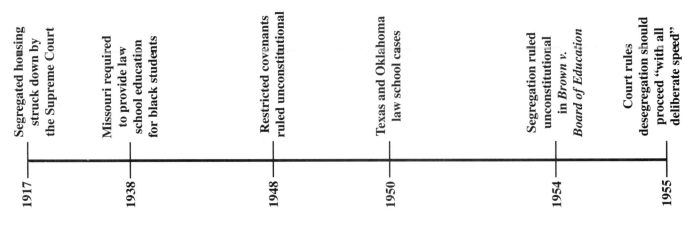

1917	1938	1948	1950	1954	1955
Segregated housing struck down by the Supreme Court	Missouri required to provide law school education for black students	Restricted covenants ruled unconstitutional	Texas and Oklahoma law school cases	Segregation ruled unconstitutional in *Brown v. Board of Education*	Court rules desegregation should proceed "with all deliberate speed"

Name: _____ Date: _____

The Landmark *Brown* Decision: Reinforcement

Directions: Complete the following activities, essays, and challenges on your own paper.

ACTIVITIES:

1. Ask the class if they feel that it was possible to end segregation all at once. Make a list of problems that approach would have met.
2. Ask the class what the difference of having a good school to attend makes on what happens to students when they grow up.

ESSAYS:

How would you answer each of these statements that someone might make?

1. "The Supreme Court did nothing to help African-Americans from 1896 to 1954."
2. "It was hard for blacks to get justice in southern courts."
3. "You don't need an education to get ahead in life."

CHALLENGES:

1. How many states had segregation laws?
2. What were "restrictive covenants"?
3. Why did the Supreme Court overturn some guilty verdicts in southern courts?
4. Why didn't African-Americans go to law school in the South?
5. Who was one of the best NAACP lawyers?
6. What area of segregation did the NAACP first tackle?
7. Name three states that lost cases in the Supreme Court because of the way they treated African-Americans who desired a legal education.
8. What was the Court's vote in *Brown v. Board of Education*?
9. What was the Court's statement in regard to *Brown v. Board of Education*?
10. In 1955, the Court said desegregation was to go forward how?

NATIONAL STANDARDS CORRELATIONS:

NCSS Vb: (Individuals, Groups, & Institutions) Analyze group and institutional influences on people, events, and elements of culture.
NSH Era 9, Standard 4: The struggle for racial and gender equality and for the extension of civil liberties

WEBSITES:

http://www.archives.gov/education/lessons/brown-v-board/
"Teaching With Documents: Documents Related to *Brown v. Board of Education*," The U.S. National Archives and Records Administration

http://www.brownvboard.org/index.htm
"In Pursuit of Freedom & Equality: *Brown v. Board of Education of Topeka*," Brown Foundation for Educational Equity, Excellence and Research

http://www.kshs.org/research/topics/cultural/brown/
"Topics in Kansas History: *Brown v. Board of Education*," Kansas State Historical Society

Moving to the Front of the Bus

Rosa Parks

The white South was not happy with school desegregation and moved with the speed of a glacier to comply. U.S. senators and representatives from the Deep South signed the "Southern Manifesto," vowing to use all lawful means to protect segregation. Their attitude was the same as that of many other whites who were determined to fight change. Separate schools was only one part of Jim Crow rule in the South. Another sign was the separation of races in transportation. African-Americans rode in separate cars on railroads and in the back seats of buses. African-Americans, strengthened by a new determination after the *Brown* decision, felt that buses, lunch counters, and other separations should also be challenged.

In the Deep South, the *Brown* decision meant nothing because people of both races felt that nothing could ever change. In Montgomery, Alabama, no one dreamed that the arrest of Rosa Parks in December 1955 had any significance at all. Mrs. Parks had worked hard all day, and she was tired. When a white man boarded the bus, the driver told her she would have to give up her seat. She refused and was arrested. Three African-American ministers of Montgomery organized a one-day boycott of city buses that continued until victory was won over a year later. Out of the boycott came the Montgomery Improvement Association (MIA), and it chose Dr. Martin Luther King, Jr., minister of the Dexter Street Baptist Church, to guide the bus boycott.

African-Americans who had never joined anything before became involved now. For many, the bus was their only way to get to work, but now they either found a ride with someone else or walked. Carpools were organized to move African-Americans around the city, and mass meetings were held to keep people enthusiastic and informed.

King's strategy was based on the concepts of Christian love and the writings of Henry David Thoreau and Mohandas (Mahatma) Gandhi on civil disobedience. His strategy was to stubbornly push toward civil rights, but to commit no act of violence that would justify white revenge. Even when his own house was bombed, he said and did nothing to provoke retaliation.

Whites did everything possible to break up the boycott. Leaders were arrested for engaging in an illegal boycott. Insurance agents refused to sell insurance to carpoolers. Police harrassed carpoolers, pulling them over for even the slightest traffic violation.

National television coverage focused on the boycott and on Dr. King, and that may have held down some white violence. After the Supreme Court held that bus segregation was illegal, African-Americans could celebrate a triumph won without white help. On December 20, 1956, Dr. King boarded a bus and sat down on a front seat. History was being made.

RESULTS: The MIA's victory proved that African-Americans could win on their own despite trying circumstances. With new confidence and spirit, African-Americans were soon challenging Jim Crow wherever he walked.

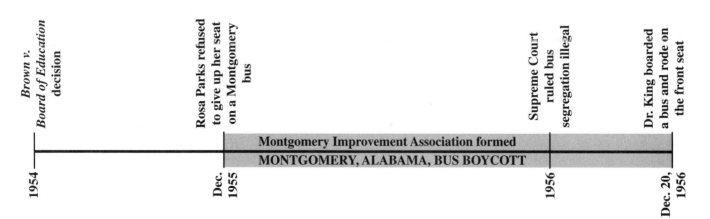

Name: _____ Date: _____

Moving to the Front of the Bus: Reinforcement

Directions: Complete the following activities, essays, and challenges on your own paper.

ACTIVITIES:

1. Ask the class why they think boycotts are effective, and why they can fail if everyone doesn't cooperate.
2. Talk about civil disobedience and the kind of courage it takes to practice it.

ESSAYS:

1. As an African-American student in Montgomery at the time, what arguments would you use to persuade a friend not to ride a bus?
2. Do you think it was Dr. King and the leaders, or was it the average African-Americans of Montgomery who deserved credit for the success? Why?
3. Why did the civil disobedience approach work in Montgomery better than a more militant approach (street demonstrations, rioting, looting)?

CHALLENGES:

1. What was the Southern Manifesto?
2. What "crime" did Mrs. Parks commit?
3. What organization led the boycott?
4. Who led the boycott?
5. What position did Martin Luther King, Jr., hold at that time?
6. What system was used to help African-Americans travel to work while the boycott was in progress?
7. What writers on civil disobedience influenced Dr. King?
8. What strategy did he use to avoid race riots?
9. What charges were brought against boycott leaders?
10. When did the boycott end? How did King celebrate the victory?

NATIONAL STANDARDS CORRELATIONS:

NCSS Xf: (Civic Ideals & Practices) Identify and explain the roles of formal and informal political actors in influencing and shaping public policy and decision-making.
NSH Era 9, Standard 4: The struggle for racial and gender equality and for the extension of civil liberties

WEBSITES:

http://memory.loc.gov/ammem/today/dec01.html
"Today in History: December 1," The Library of Congress

http://www.africanaonline.com/montgomery.htm
"Montgomery Bus Boycott," Africanaonline by Toonari

http://www.stanford.edu/group/King/about_king/encyclopedia/bus_boycott.html
"Montgomery Bus Boycott," Martin Luther King, Jr., Papers Project

http://www.archives.state.al.us/teacher/rights/lesson1/doc1.html
"Montgomery City Code," Alabama Department of Archives & History

Desegregating Little Rock Central High

The Supreme Court's decision in *Brown v. Board of Education of Topeka* allowed school districts to work with federal district judges to design desegregation plans. The Little Rock, Arkansas, school board decided to desegregate Central High School in 1957, junior highs in 1960, and elementary schools in 1963. The judge approved the plan, and nine African-American students were selected to attend Central High School in September.

Up until 1957, desegregation had moved quietly in Arkansas. Governor Orval Faubus had done nothing to stop it, but after a delegation of white mothers visited him, Faubus announced that he was going to call out the National Guard to "prevent violence" and the nine students from entering the school. President Eisenhower at first was reluctant to act, noting that laws do not change

students being escorted into High School

people's hearts. The federal judge, however, did not hesitate in overruling the governor, and Faubus withdrew the guardsmen, leaving protection of the nine students to the Little Rock police.

Each day, the nine students were greeted by a howling mob. Eisenhower warned that he was prepared to use "whatever force may be necessary to enforce the law." Few of the protesters were from Little Rock. They came from all over the South to show their hatred for federal court orders and African-Americans. Inside the building, the African-American students were harassed in the halls and cafeteria. Only careful training prevented them from foolish responses that would destroy their reason for being there. When the situation became impossible, the police took them out a back door to waiting cars. It appeared for a time that the mob was winning the battle in the streets.

Television cameras recorded events at Little Rock each day. Many whites in Little Rock were embarrassed and wanted the demonstrations ended. The president and the nation had also had enough. Eisenhower federalized the Arkansas National Guard on September 24 and sent 1,000 federal troops to Little Rock. Despite protests by southern senators and governors, Eisenhower refused to pull federal troops out until Faubus gave assurances that the court order would be completely complied with, and the situation became peaceful enough that the police could maintain order without difficulty. In November, all federal troops were withdrawn, but 900 guardsmen remained.

In 1958, Faubus closed Little Rock schools and tried to lease the buildings to a newly formed school corporation, but that approach was rejected by the U.S. Court of Appeals. By May 1959, tempers flared as whites willing to desegregate clashed with CROSS (Committee to Retain Our Segregated Schools). After the Supreme Court ruled that the law closing schools was unconstitutional, six African-American students enrolled with whites: three at Central High and three at Hall High.

RESULTS: For the first time in 80 years, a president used federal troops to enforce civil rights. For African-Americans, this was a sign of changing times.

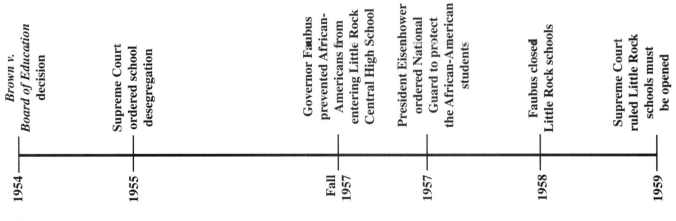

Timeline:
- 1954 — *Brown v. Board of Education* decision
- 1955 — Supreme Court ordered school desegregation
- Fall 1957 — Governor Faubus prevented African-Americans from entering Little Rock Central High School
- 1957 — President Eisenhower ordered National Guard to protect the African-American students
- 1958 — Faubus closed Little Rock schools
- 1959 — Supreme Court ruled Little Rock schools must be opened

Name: _____ Date: _____

Desegregating Little Rock Central High: Reinforcement

Directions: Complete the following activities, essays, and challenges on your own paper.

ACTIVITIES:

1. Discuss the pressures the nine students must have felt.
2. Ask if the class thinks Eisenhower was right to bring in outside troops rather than depend solely on National Guard units.

ESSAYS:

1. Do you agree with the statement that "laws do not change people's hearts"? Why or why not?
2. As one of the African-American students selected for this "opportunity," would you have accepted? Why or why not?
3. Do you think that the situation at Little Rock was beneficial in the long run for the civil rights movement? Why or why not?

CHALLENGES:

1. Who worked with school boards in designing desegregation policies?
2. Who was the governor of Arkansas in 1957?
3. Why was Eisenhower unhappy with the court's desegregation policy?
4. What did Faubus do after he was overruled by the federal judge?
5. Who vowed to use "whatever force may be necessary to enforce the law"?
6. What did Eisenhower do to restore order?
7. What terms did Eisenhower give Faubus before ordering federal troops to leave?
8. How did Faubus try to get around the federal judge?
9. What did the Court of Appeals do then?
10. What did the initials "CROSS" stand for?

NATIONAL STANDARDS CORRELATIONS:

<u>NCSS Xf:</u> (Civic Ideals & Practices) Identify and explain the roles of formal and informal political actors in influencing and shaping public policy and decision-making.
<u>NSH Era 9, Standard 4:</u> The struggle for racial and gender equality and for the extension of civil liberties

WEBSITES:

http://www.ardemgaz.com/prev/central/
"Historic Front Pages From the *Arkansas Democrat* and *Arkansas Gazette*," Little Rock Newspapers

http://www.cr.nps.gov/nr/travel/civilrights/ak1.htm
"Little Rock Central High School National Historic Site," National Park Service

http://www.cr.nps.gov/nr/twhp/wwwlps/lessons/crandall/CRfacts2.htm
"Reading 2: All Eyes on Little Rock Central High," National Park Service

http://www.eisenhower.archives.gov/dl/LittleRock/littlerockdocuments.html
"Little Rock School Integration Crisis," The Dwight D. Eisenhower Library

The Civil Rights Movement

Martin Luther King, Jr. giving speech

The victory over segregated buses in Montgomery gave Dr. Martin Luther King, Jr., a national platform from which to speak. His message struck a chord with many northern whites, as well as most southern African-Americans. Using the Southern Christian Leadership Conference (SCLC) he had formed as his base, King moved against many strongholds of segregation. In 1960, he was jailed in Atlanta for his protests against discrimination at a department store.

Others were also at work. Four African-American college students started a sit-in at a Greensboro, North Carolina, lunch counter, and within two weeks, there were sit-ins in 15 cities in five southern states. They suffered many attacks and abuses by angry whites, but their resolve drew new recruits. In 1960, they organized as the Student Nonviolent Coordinating Committee (SNCC).

Another group that was active was the Congress Of Racial Equality (CORE), which targeted segregation on interstate buses. In 1956, the Interstate Commerce Commission (ICC) ordered an end to segregation on buses and trains crossing state lines, but it was a long way from Washington to Alabama. In the Deep South, drivers continued to insist that African-Americans move to the back of the bus. In 1961, CORE sent "Freedom Riders" into the South. White and African-American supporters sat on buses next to each other and refused to separate. Sometimes angry mobs gathered at bus stations and brutally attacked the riders.

In 1963, Dr. King was arrested in Birmingham after defying Police Chief Eugene "Bull" Connor by staging a demonstration. While King was being held, he wrote his famous "Letter from Birmingham City Jail" in response to critics who accused him of being there to stir up trouble. He wrote that his approach was "to create ... such creative tension that a community that has constantly refused to negotiate is forced to confront the issue."

That summer, Medgar Evers, field secretary of the Mississippi NAACP, was shot and killed in front of his home. This caused protests in a number of cities, and President Kennedy said in a television address, "We face, therefore, a moral crisis as a country and as a people."

Civil rights leaders united to create a "March on Washington" in August 1963, and over 200,000 were part of the largest demonstration of its kind in American history. The highlight came when Dr. King addressed the audience with his "I Have a Dream" speech. King said the civil rights effort would continue "until justice rolls down like the waters and righteousness like a mighty stream." Then he said, "I have a dream that someday, in the red hills of Georgia, the sons of former slaves and slaveowners will sit at the table of brotherhood." And someday, he said, all will join hands and sing, "Free at last, free at last; thank God Almighty, we are free at last."

RESULTS: The "I Have a Dream" speech mobilized public opinion in an amazing way, and it gave the civil rights movement added stature.

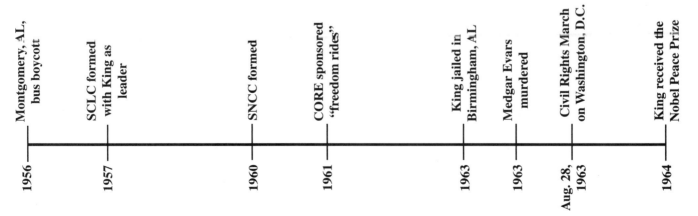

Name: _____ Date: _____

The Civil Rights Movement: Reinforcement

Directions: Complete the following activities, essays, and challenges on your own paper.

ACTIVITIES:

1. Listen to an audio recording or view a video recording of the "I Have a Dream" speech.
2. Ask the class why they think it was important to King to have a peaceful march on Washington.

ESSAYS:

1. What do you think was most important about the March on Washington? Was it because of the size of the crowd or the speeches?
2. What do you think King meant by "creative tension"? How could a person today use it to good advantage?
3. Why do you think so many civil rights groups were at work in the early 1960s?

CHALLENGES:

1. What were the initials of Martin Luther King, Jr.'s organization?
2. Where was the first lunch counter demonstration?
3. What were the initials of the civil rights movement that was formed in 1960?
4. What group worked to end segregation on interstate buses?
5. What were the white and African-American riders called?
6. Who wrote "Letter from Birmingham City Jail"?
7. What job did Medgar Evers have before he was killed?
8. Who said: "We face a moral crisis"?
9. When was the March on Washington, and how many participated?
10. Who gave the famous "I Have a Dream" speech?

NATIONAL STANDARDS CORRELATIONS:

NCSS Xf: (Civic Ideals & Practices) Identify and explain the roles of formal and informal political actors in influencing and shaping public policy and decision-making.
NSH Era 9, Standard 4: The struggle for racial and gender equality and for the extension of civil liberties

WEBSITES:

http://memory.loc.gov/ammem/aaohtml/exhibit/aopart9.html
"The Civil Rights Era," The Library of Congress

http://memory.loc.gov/ammam/today/mar07.html
"Today in History: March 7," The Library of Congress

http://www.stanford.edu/group/King/about_king/encyclopedia/
"King Encyclopedia," Martin Luther King, Jr., Papers Project

http://www.cr.nps.gov/nr/travel/civilrights/
"Historic Places of the Civil Rights Movement: We Shall Overcome," National Park Service

Radical Movements

Malcolm X

To many Americans, the mid-1960s was a period when the traditional America was falling apart. After the murders of Medgar Evers and President John Kennedy, racial and generational gaps began to appear everywhere, and Americans debated everything from Afro-haircuts to women's issues to youth culture. African-Americans argued about which policies should be followed and which should be ignored.

Many African-Americans thought the King approach was too slow and too devoted to winning white approval. They were impatient and wanted change NOW! An example of this occurred when the Student Nonviolent Coordinating Committee (SNCC) elected Stokely Carmichael as president and removed whites from membership. Carmichael said in 1966, "We have got to get us some *Black Power*." A term had been born that others would use often.

Northern African-Americans, many living in ghettos and public housing projects, were as segregated as Southern African-Americans, except their separation was *de facto* segregation (separation in reality), while Southern African-Americans could attack Jim Crow laws (*de jure* segregation). Many African-Americans worked to achieve the American dream and to be accepted as equals, but others were more interested in developing a separate African-American community with its own lifestyle–a nation within a nation. The stress was on African roots and pride in being African-American. African-American novelists, poets, artists, and leaders were studied, and Richard Wright's *Native Son,* Ralph Ellison's *Invisible Man,* and James Baldwin's *Go Tell It on the Mountain* were read by many African-Americans and whites.

One group became well known for wanting complete separation from white America. Elijah Muhammad's Black Muslim movement had been formed in the 1930s, but had never attracted much attention until the 1960s. The Black Muslim lifestyle required clean living (no tobacco or alcohol). Stressing the need for economic power, the Black Muslims ran a variety of businesses, including department stores, restaurants, and farms. Two of the most famous converts were Malcolm X and the heavyweight champion Cassius Clay, who changed his name to Muhammad Ali.

Malcolm Little was in prison when he converted to the Black Muslims and changed his name to Malcolm X. A powerful public speaker, he quickly rose in the organization to become better known than Elijah Muhammad. In 1963, he clashed with Elijah Muhammad and was removed from the Black Muslims. After a trip to Mecca, he rejected the Black Muslim doctrine that all whites were evil, and he established the Organization of Afro-American Unity to fight white racism. He was killed in 1965 by two Black Muslims, just before his book, *The Autobiography of Malcolm X,* was published.

RESULTS: The issue of separatism vs. integration continued to divide the African-American community and perplex the whites. Unless action was taken, radical solutions would divide the nation even more than it already was.

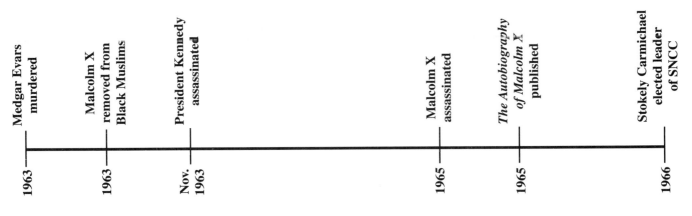

Name: _____ Date: _____

Radical Movements: Reinforcement

Directions: Complete the following activities, essays, and challenges on your own paper.

ACTIVITIES:

1. Stage a discussion between a white who has been kicked out of the Student Nonviolent Coordinating Committee (SNCC) and the person who has removed him from its membership roll.
2. Discuss the phrase "Black Power," and ask the students how the phrase might be interpreted by various African-American leaders of the 1960s.

ESSAYS:

1. Which is harder to fight: *de jure* or *de facto* segregation? Why?
2. What is the difference between what Martin Luther King and Elijah Muhammad wanted? Which do you think was right? Why?
3. After researching Malcolm X, list five questions you would ask him in an interview, and tell why you would ask them.

CHALLENGES:

1. What were some criticisms of King's approach?
2. What membership change did the Student Nonviolent Coordinating Committee (SNCC) make?
3. Who first used the phrase "Black Power"?
4. What is meant by *de facto* segregation?
5. Who wrote *Native Son*?
6. Who wrote *Invisible Man*?
7. What products did Black Muslims refuse to use?
8. Who were the most famous Black Muslim converts?
9. What were three types of businesses run by Black Muslims?
10. Malcolm X was the founder of what organization?

NATIONAL STANDARDS CORRELATIONS:

NCSS Xf: (Civic Ideals & Practices) Identify and explain the roles of formal and informal political actors in influencing and shaping public policy and decision-making.
NSH Era 9, Standard 4: The struggle for racial and gender equality and for the extension of civil liberties

WEBSITES:

http://www.cmgww.com/historic/malcolm/about/bio.htm
"About Malcolm X: Biography," Estate of Malcolm X

http://www.brothermalcolm.net/
"Malcolm X: A Research Site," University of Toledo and Twenty-First Century Books

http://foia.fbi.gov/foiaindex/bmuslims.htm
"Black Muslims," Federal Bureau of Investigation

http://www.stg.brown.edu/projects/FreedomNow/themes/blkpower/index.html
"Republic of New Africa," Brown University and Tougaloo College

The Civil and Voting Rights Acts

College students at sit-in

Eisenhower had pushed the Civil Rights Act of 1957 through Congress. It gave the federal government the power to take cases to court where a person's right to vote was denied or threatened. Instead of that person or the NAACP paying the legal fees, the government would pay the expense. Many were not impressed with this and saw the need for a stronger law.

Kennedy's civil rights proposals were more ambitious, but he was frustrated by southern Democrats who led Congress. Still, he was willing to take some political risks. In 1962, he sent troops to protect James Meredith, the first African-American student to enroll at the University of Mississippi. When Governor George Wallace tried to prevent three African-Americans from enrolling at the University of Alabama in 1963, Kennedy forced the governor to step aside. The assassination of President Kennedy caused the same shock among African-Americans as it did among whites. African-Americans feared that the new president, Lyndon B. Johnson, would be less active on their behalf.

Johnson lacked Kennedy's public appeal, but he understood Congress and knew how to get bills through. One of his early accomplishments was the Civil Rights Act of 1964. It made it illegal to discriminate in public places (restaurants, hotels, bus stations, barber shops, etc.) against anyone on the basis of race. It also attacked job discrimination. It did not end the problems African-Americans had in traveling or finding a job, but it was the beginning of new opportunities for African-Americans to be treated as customers and workers deserving proper respect.

In the South, voting remained as a big problem. Difficult literacy tests, odd hours and days for registering to vote, and a long history of never having voted discouraged African-American participation. Dr. King and other leaders realized that voting power could change the way white officials treated African-Americans and the way African-Americans looked at themselves. To call attention to the problems African-Americans had in registering to vote, Dr. King focused his efforts on Selma, Alabama, in February 1965. Demonstrators met the strong arm of state troopers and sheriff's deputies.

On March 7, King and about 600 others started a march of the 54 miles between Selma and the state capital of Montgomery. They were attacked by 200 troopers and deputized posse members using tear gas, whips, and nightsticks. Seventeen African-Americans were injured while TV cameras recorded the event. When the march resumed on March 17, it was protected by soldiers.

A Voting Rights Act passed in Congress in 1965, ending most literacy tests and giving the U.S. attorney-general the power to appoint voting registrars in counties where it appeared to him that local officials were not letting African-Americans register.

RESULTS: The full effect of the Civil Rights Act would not be felt at first, but thanks to the Voting Rights Act, thousands of African-Americans all over the South became voters in a very short time.

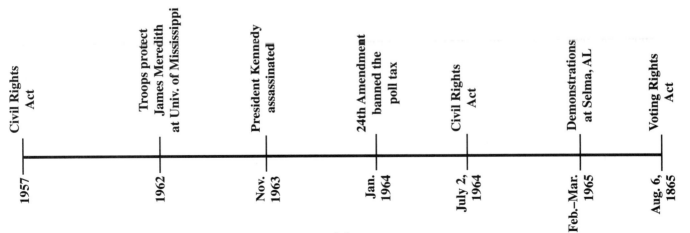

Civil Rights Act — 1957

Troops protect James Meredith at Univ. of Mississippi — 1962

President Kennedy assassinated — Nov. 1963

24th Amendment banned the poll tax — Jan. 1964

Civil Rights Act — July 2, 1964

Demonstrations at Selma, AL — Feb.–Mar. 1965

Voting Rights Act — Aug. 6, 1865

Name: _____ Date: _____

The Civil and Voting Rights Acts: Reinforcement

Directions: Complete the following activities, essays, and challenges on your own paper.

ACTIVITIES:

1. If it is available, play a portion of *Eyes on the Prize* for your class to let them see and feel some of the excitement of the mid-1960s.
2. Ask why southern white leaders of the time were so strongly against letting African-Americans vote.

ESSAYS:

1. Why is the Civil Rights Act still important to minorities and women?
2. Why was voting so important to African-Americans in the 1960s?
3. As a northern African-American of that time, what did these two laws mean to you? Why?

CHALLENGES:

1. What law gave the attorney-general power to bring civil rights cases to court?
2. Who was the first African-American student to attend the University of Mississippi?
3. Who tried to prevent three African-American students from attending the University of Alabama?
4. What law required restaurants to serve African-Americans?
5. In what ways did voting registrars in the South try to discourage African-Americans from voting?
6. In what town did voting rights become a national issue?
7. How far was the march from Selma to Montgomery?
8. How many were involved in the Selma-Montgomery march; what happened to the first group?
9. What was the major difference in the marches on the 7th and 17th of March 1965?
10. What was included in the Voting Rights Act?

NATIONAL STANDARDS CORRELATIONS:

NCSS Xa: (Civic Ideals & Practices) Examine the origins and continuing influence of key ideals of the democratic republican form of government, such as individual human dignity, liberty, justice, equality, and the rule of law.
NSH Era 9, Standard 4: The struggle for racial and gender equality and for the extension of civil liberties

WEBSITES:

http://www.archives.gov/education/lessons/civil-rights-act/
"Teaching With Documents: The Civil Rights Act of 1964 and the Equal Employment Opportunity Commission," The U.S. National Archives and Records Administration

http://www.vcdh.virginia.edu/solguide/VUS13/VUS13.html
"The Civil Rights Movement," Virginia Center for Digital History

http://www.yale.edu/lawweb/avalon/statutes/voting_rights_1965.htm
"Voting Rights Act of 1965; August 6, 1965," The Avalon Project at Yale Law School

http://usinfo.state.gov/usa/infousa/laws/majorlaw/civilr19.htm
"Civil Rights Act of 1964," U.S. Department of State

Pain and Trouble in the Late 1960s

It is difficult to describe the 1960s, because so many things were happening. Johnson's victory over Goldwater was won with the nearly unanimous support of African-Americans. The president's programs, like Head Start and Medicare, were helpful to those in the youngest and oldest age groups. His appointment of Thurgood Marshall to the Supreme Court was especially pleasing to African-Americans; now, one of the brothers was one of the Brethren (as Supreme Court justices are sometimes called). With its emphasis on protecting the rights of defendants, the Court became much more strict about arrest procedures and trials of the poor and minorities.

Blacks prevented from entering segregated theater

However, President Johnson's popularity suffered among African-Americans and whites. His Great Society programs were often badly managed. The Office of Economic Opportunity (OEO) ran many idealistic programs that did not work and were very costly. Public Housing projects irritated both those who dwelt there and taxpayers alike. However, Johnson's greatest cause of unpopularity was the Vietnam War. With the increased draft came the criticism that whites with money went to college or Canada, and the poor and minorities went to Vietnam.

The black civil rights movement was now only one of many protests out on the street or on the university campus. Women, anti-war demonstrators, and other minority groups were also holding rallies. Police tolerance for protests sometimes ran thin, and tempers ran high on all sides. TV networks had a hard time deciding which group's protests deserved top billing on the evening news. This caused those seeking public attention to become more outspoken and colorful.

The Black Panther party was formed by Huey Newton and Bobby Seale, who believed the police oppressed the residents of African-American neighborhoods; the Panther solution was arming the people to protect themselves. Eldridge Cleaver, author of *Soul on Ice,* joined the Panthers and pushed revolutionary doctrines. Panthers were often accused of terrorist acts, and there were several shootouts with police. In time, the Panthers changed and shifted toward programs to help: school breakfasts and voter registration. By the mid-1970s, the Panthers had disappeared.

Urban race riots spread as African-Americans showed their anger with existing conditions. These were often sparked by a small incident—an arrest, the turning off of a fire hydrant, or an assault on an individual. To find out why riots occurred, Johnson appointed the Kerner Commission to look into the causes. It reported in 1968 that the most important causes were police practices, unemployment and underemployment, and poor housing. The Commission Report warned, "Our nation is moving toward two societies, one black, one white—separate but unequal."

RESULTS: When Dr. King was killed by a white racist in 1968, many Americans went into a time of mourning and self-examination, but the period of rioting in cities caused others to support get-tough policies.

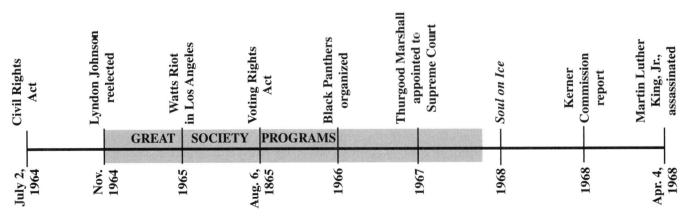

Civil Rights Act	Lyndon Johnson reelected	Watts Riot in Los Angeles	Voting Rights Act	Black Panthers organized	Thurgood Marshall appointed to Supreme Court	Soul on Ice	Kerner Commission report	Martin Luther King, Jr., assassinated

GREAT SOCIETY PROGRAMS

| July 2, 1964 | Nov. 1964 | 1965 | Aug. 6, 1865 | 1966 | 1967 | 1968 | 1968 | Apr. 4, 1968 |

Name: _____ Date: _____

Pain and Trouble in the Late 1960s: Reinforcement

Directions: Complete the following activities, essays, and challenges on your own paper.

ACTIVITIES:

1. From what the class understands about the nation's ghettos, ask what they think causes riots.
2. Ask the class why they think that revolutionary groups like the Black Panthers change over the years.

ESSAYS:

1. Dr. King toured one riot area and was told by one rioter, "We won." He asked how they could think they had won when the neighborhood was in flames and there were no stores left. The looter said, "We won because we made them pay attention to us." How would you have answered if you had been Dr. King?
2. Why was it difficult for groups like the NAACP and Urban League to get much attention in the 1960s?
3. Early statements of the Black Panthers were much more radical than the statements of the 1970s. Why do you think they changed?

CHALLENGES:

1. What was the program to help preschool children called?
2. What African-American was selected for the Supreme Court?
3. What did the initials OEO stand for?
4. Why were African-Americans and other minorities unhappy over the war in Vietnam?
5. Who were the founders of the Black Panthers?
6. Who joined the Black Panthers later?
7. What kinds of projects did the Black Panthers take on in the 1970s?
8. What was the Kerner Commission created to do?
9. What were some of the causes of the riots found in the Commission's investigation?
10. What was the warning that was included in the Kerner Commission Report in regard to our nation's society?

NATIONAL STANDARDS CORRELATIONS:

NCSS Xf: (Civic Ideals & Practices) Identify and explain the roles of formal and informal political actors in influencing and shaping public policy and decision-making.
NSH Era 9, Standard 4: The struggle for racial and gender equality and for the extension of civil liberties

WEBSITES:

http://www.pbs.org/hueypnewton/huey.html
"A Huey P. Newton Story," Public Broadcasting Service

http://www.stanford.edu/group/blackpanthers/history.shtml
"History of the Black Panther Party," Black Panther Party Research Project

http://www.oyez.org/oyez/resource/legal_entity/96/overview
"Thurgood Marshall," The Oyez Project

http://memory.loc.gov/ammem/today/oct02.html
"Today in History: October 2," The Library of Congress

African-Americans Move to the City

The "Black Power" of the 1960s was met by "Backlash Power" in the 1970s, as whites turned against social programs. Richard Nixon, in 1968, opposed busing to achieve integration and was supported by only 13 percent of African-Americans. George Wallace, the third-party candidate, attacked school integration and welfare mothers. Vice President Hubert Humphrey, the Democratic candidate, had long supported liberal causes, but white voters associated him with unpopular Johnson policies. The election was not limited to race; there were many domestic and foreign policy issues, including the Vietnam war. Although Nixon barely defeated Humphrey in popular vote, the combined Nixon-Wallace vote amounted to 56.9 percent of votes cast.

Downtown Manhattan Skyline

The Civil Rights Act of 1968 attempted to help African-Americans by outlawing discrimination based on race, color, religion, national origin, or sex. Among the things it had made illegal were the practices of some real estate agents and banks: steering, redlining, and block busting. *Steering* was showing African-Americans houses only in African-American neighborhoods. *Block busting* was selling a house to an African-American in a white neighborhood, then panicking white residents in the area to sell their homes at a lower price; the agents then sold the homes to African-Americans, but at a higher price. *Redlining* was when a bank refused to lend to homebuyers in neighborhoods changing from white to African-American.

This law was of little use in solving the problem of racial segregation. "White flight"—the moving of whites from the cities to suburbs—was causing cities to become more African-American and was leaving few whites behind to integrate with African-Americans. Newark, New Jersey, was 34 percent African-American in 1960 and 58 percent African-American in 1980. Detroit was about 29 percent African-American in 1960 and 63 percent African-American in 1980. Hartford, Connecticut, went from 15 percent to 34 percent African-American in that same time period. Washington, D.C., went from 54 percent African-American to 70 percent. Atlanta went from 38 percent to 66 percent. Many other cities were not changing as much, but the trend was toward more African-Americans and less whites in cities.

If cities were the place where dreams came true for African-Americans in the 1920s and 1940s, they were no longer that by the 1980s. If cities were where jobs were, and if they were not suffering from the old age of their streets, bridges, sewers, and water systems (infrastructure), the change from white to African-American would have benefited African-Americans. But cities were showing signs of decay in housing and infrastructure. The industrial jobs left northern cities and moved to the "Sunbelt" in the south and west. New factories in the north were being built outside cities. City school systems were competing with wealthier suburbs for good teachers, and they could not match them in wages and classroom size.

RESULTS: Ever since the Chicago *Defender* had encouraged African-Americans to go north in the early twentieth century, African-Americans had moved to cities with great expectations. Those arriving from the 1960s to the 1980s found cities to be centers of high unemployment and social problems.

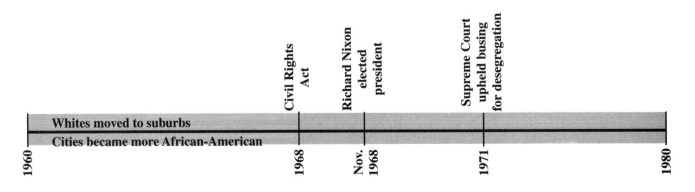

Name: _____ Date: _____

African-Americans Move to the City: Reinforcement

Directions: Complete the following activities, essays, and challenges on your own paper.

ACTIVITIES:

1. Have the students look at a map of your town or city. Are there certain parts of the city that are predominately white or African-American residential areas?
2. To make sure they understand what the term means, ask the class to list problems faced by your town or city in the way of infrastructure.

ESSAYS:

1. What is meant by "backlash"? Give an example of how it might apply to your life.
2. Less federal money was spent on cities in the 1970s. As an African-American politician of the time, what would you give as the reasons?
3. Cities were losing tax revenues in the 1970s. As a city official of the time, would you have favored raising taxes on industries in your city?

CHALLENGES:

1. What Nixon policy angered African-Americans?
2. What did Wallace often attack?
3. What law outlawed various forms of discrimination?
4. What was the term used when an African-American couple was only shown houses in African-American neighborhoods?
5. What was the term used when whites were frightened into selling their homes, and real estate agents then sold the houses at inflated prices to African-Americans?
6. What was the term used when a bank refused to lend to homebuyers in changing neighborhoods?
7. What was meant by "white flight"?
8. Of the five cities mentioned, which changed the most in increased African-American percentage of population?
9. Which of the five cities changed least?
10. What is the collective term used for a city's streets, bridges, and sewers?

NATIONAL STANDARDS CORRELATIONS:

NCSS IIIh: (People, Places, & Environments) Examine, interpret, and analyze physical and cultural patterns and their interactions, such as land use, settlement patterns, cultural transmission of customs and ideas, and ecosystem changes.
NSH Era 9, Standard 4: The struggle for racial and gender equality and for the extension of civil liberties

WEBSITES:

http://www.hud.gov/offices/fheo/aboutfheo/history.cfm
"Celebrating Fair Housing," U.S. Department of Housing and Urban Development

http://www.liu.edu/cwis/cwp/library/african/2000/1980.htm
"African-Americans in the Twentieth Century: 1980," Long Island University

http://www.nixonera.com/library/domestic.asp
"Re-evaluating Richard Nixon: his domestic achievements by Joan Hoff," The Nixon Era Center at Mountain State University

Rising African-American Influence in Politics

When Hiram Revels and Blanche Bruce went to the Senate in the 1870s, African-Americans had their first real voice in national affairs; but critics said it was only because of Reconstruction. When Booker T. Washington ate lunch at the White House in 1901, it caused a great public outcry; but it was said that he was unique. Oscar DePriest's election to the House of Representatives in the 1920s was the first signal that African-Americans could gain political power on their own.

African-Americans have risen to influence in Congress and have held important positions. Adam Clayton Powell chaired the House Committee on Education and Labor in the 1960s. Charles Rangel chaired the Select Committee on Narcotics. William Gray served as the House majority whip. Edward Brooke served as a senator from Massachusetts. Powerful political roles have been held by Congresswomen: Shirley Chisholm and Barbara Jordan served as U.S. representatives, and in 1992, Carol Mosley Braun was elected to the Senate.

Jesse Jackson

African-Americans have served as presidential advisors and in key political policy-making positions. Dr. Mary McCleod Bethune advised Presidents Franklin D. Roosevelt and Harry S Truman. Patricia Roberts Harris was secretary of Health, Education, and Welfare in 1979. Carl Rowan became the director of the United States Information Agency (USIA) in 1964, and Benjamin Hooks was the first African-American to serve on the Federal Communications Commission (FCC). Andrew Brimmer was the first African-American on the Federal Reserve Board. The first African-American chairman of the Democratic National Committee was Ron Brown. After the 1992 election, Vernon Jordan was named to head President-elect Bill Clinton's transition team. Colin Powell, who had been the first African-American national security advisor under Ronald Reagan, became President George W. Bush's secretary of state. Condoleezza Rice was the first African-American woman to be the national security advisor. President Bush then appointed her as secretary of state when Colin Powell stepped down.

Serving as diplomats have been Dr. Ralph Bunche, Donald McHenry, and Andrew Young in the United Nations. Bunche received a Nobel Peace Prize for his work as United Nations undersecretary. African-Americans have served as ambassadors to many nations.

In the judicial branch, two African-Americans have served on the U.S. Supreme Court: Thurgood Marshall and Clarence Thomas. Wade McCree, Jr., was the U.S. solicitor general (the person who argues the federal cases before the Supreme Court). Others have served as judges on courts of appeals, as federal district court judges, and U.S. attorneys.

Douglas Wilder's election as governor of Virginia made him the most important African-American state official. A number of cities have elected African-American mayors. Those who broke the color line first included Maynard Jackson (Atlanta), Ernest Morial (New Orleans), Thomas Bradley (Los Angeles), Harold Washington (Chicago), and David Dinkins (New York City).

In 1984 and 1988, Jesse Jackson ran for president with the support of his "Rainbow Coalition." He was unsuccessful in gaining the nomination, but he inspired many African-Americans to register and run for public office.

RESULTS: There are three times as many African-American legislators and four times as many city and county officials today than there were in 1970. This is a sign that African-Americans are becoming more politically aware and active.

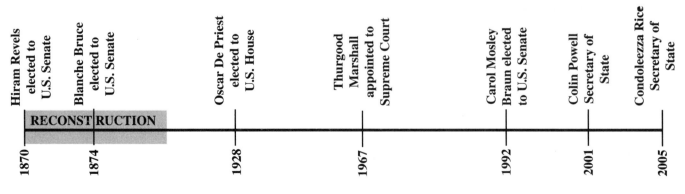

| Hiram Revels elected to U.S. Senate | Blanche Bruce elected to U.S. Senate | Oscar De Priest elected to U.S. House | Thurgood Marshall appointed to Supreme Court | Carol Mosley Braun elected to U.S. Senate | Colin Powell Secretary of State | Condoleezza Rice Secretary of State |

RECONSTRUCTION

| 1870 | 1874 | 1928 | 1967 | 1992 | 2001 | 2005 |

Name: _____   Date: _____

Rising African-American Influence in Politics: Reinforcement

Directions: Complete the following activities, essays, and challenges on your own paper.

ACTIVITIES:

1. Look for articles in newspapers and magazines about African-Americans who are prominent in government.
2. Debate the question of whether an African-American will ever become president or vice president, with students presenting arguments pro and con.

ESSAYS:

1. If you were giving advice to your party's presidential nominee, what African-American would you recommend for vice president, and why?
2. Why is it important to African-Americans to know that African-Americans have been elected or appointed to key positions in government?
3. What qualities do you think are necessary for an African-American man or woman to succeed in rising up the political ladder?

CHALLENGES:

1. Who chaired the House Committee on Education and Labor in the 1960s?
2. Who was the first African-American secretary of state?
3. Who was the first African-American in the Senate since Reconstruction?
4. Name two important women who served in Congress.
5. Who was President George W. Bush's national security advisor?
6. Who was the first African-American person to serve as chairman of a national party?
7. What undersecretary of the United Nations received the Nobel Peace Prize?
8. What are the names of two African-Americans who have served on the Supreme Court?
9. Who was the first African-American person elected governor of Virginia?
10. Who formed the "Rainbow Coalition" in his efforts to win the Democratic nomination for president?

NATIONAL STANDARDS CORRELATIONS:

NCSS Xf: (Civic Ideals & Practices) Identify and explain the roles of formal and informal political actors in influencing and shaping public policy and decision-making.

NSH Era 10, Standard 2: Economic, social, and cultural developments in the contemporary United States

WEBSITES:

http://bioguide.congress.gov/scripts/biodisplay.pl?index=B000968
"Bruce, Blanche Kelso, (1841–1898)," Biographical Directory of the United States Congress

http://bioguide.congress.gov/scripts/biodisplay.pl?index=R000166
"Revels, Hiram Rhodes, (1827–1901)," Biographical Directory of the United States Congress

http://www.rainbowpush.org/founder/
"The Reverend Jesse Louis Jackson, Sr., Founder and President: Rainbow/PUSH Coalition," Rainbow/Push Coalition

http://www.supremecourthistory.org/myweb/justice/thomas.htm
"Clarence Thomas," Supreme Court Historical Society

Sports and Entertainment

Jackie Robinson

In the summer of 1992, athletes from many nations gathered at Barcelona, Spain, to compete in the Olympics. What made it so unusual was the presence of the "dream team," which included many superstars of the NBA: men like Michael Jordan and Magic Johnson—the team's performance left no doubt of African-American importance in basketball. There were many track stars as well, including Jackie Joyner-Kersee, who has set many world records, despite suffering asthma attacks.

When Jack Johnson won the heavyweight boxing championship in 1908, Jesse Owens won in the 1936 Olympics, Jackie Robinson was selected as the National League MVP in 1949, and tennis players Althea Gibson and Arthur Ashe won at Wimbledon in 1957 and 1975 respectively, the African-American role in sports began to be important if not dominant. The names and faces of athletes change quickly, but it would require great imagination to think of professional football, basketball, and baseball without African-American athletes in key roles and as a large percentage of team composition.

The portrayal of African-Americans in movies and television has changed dramatically. In early movies, African-Americans were either shiftless comic relief or servants. Some became well-known. Hattie McDaniel won an Oscar for her role as mammy to Scarlett O'Hara in *Gone with the Wind.* Luther "Bojangles" Robinson was a tap dancer often appearing in Shirley Temple movies. After World War II, African-American actors were given better roles in movies, and stars like Sidney Poitier began to make their mark. Movies focusing on African-Americans have included such important films as *Raisin in the Sun, The Color Purple,* and *Glory.* In 2002, for the first time, both the Oscars for leading actor and actress went to African-American performers: Denzel Washington and Halle Berry.

Radio, and later television, made little use of African-American actors at first. The most recognizable voice of an African-American actor in radio was that of Eddie "Rochester" Anderson, who got big laughs as Jack Benny's valet. The first African-American star on television was Bill Cosby, who won the Emmy for his role in the *I Spy* series in 1966. His successful *The Cosby Show,* the story of the Huxtable family, became a landmark in television history. By the end of the 1980s, many television shows had included African-Americans in either the major or important supporting roles. The miniseries of Alex Haley's *Roots* captured high reviews and Nielsen ratings. In 1988, *The Cosby Show* and *A Different World* ranked as the No. 1 and No. 2 rated shows on television.

The African-American role in music has become a major part of the entertainment industry as well, and the African-American presence is visible in popular music, in addition to many other forms. In classical music, for instance, Marian Anderson and Leontyne Price stand out. Harry Belafonte made calypso music popular in America. Rap and hip-hop music is largely based on African-American urban culture.

RESULTS: The role of African-Americans in sports and show business plays a major part in American life today, and generally, it improves the African-American image.

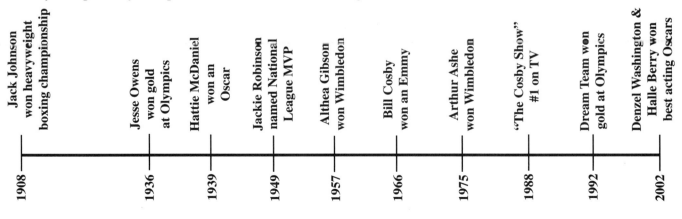

Name: _____   Date: _____

Sports and Entertainment: Reinforcement

Directions: Complete the following activities, essays, and challenges on your own paper.

ACTIVITIES:

1. Make a list of African-American athletes, actors, and singers who are especially successful today. Ask the class what makes them successful.
2. Have a class watch a TV show that has African-Americans as its theme. Ask them to decide whether the images it gives to the general public are good or bad.

ESSAYS:

1. Do you think that the success of an African-American athlete today is as important to African-Americans as it once was?
2. Why do you think African-American actors and actresses had so much trouble getting good roles in movies?
3. Who, in your opinion, is the best African-American entertainer today? Why do you think so?

CHALLENGES:

1. Name two members of the "dream team."
2. Who became the first African-American "Most Valuable Player" in the National League?
3. Name two highly successful African-American tennis players.
4. What African-American actress won an Oscar for her role in *Gone with the Wind?*
5. What African-American dancer often appeared in Shirley Temple movies?
6. Who played Rochester on the Jack Benny radio shows?
7. Name a movie portraying the African-American experience.
8. Who wrote the *Roots* miniseries?
9. What was the No. 1 rated TV show in 1988?
10. What singer made calypso music popular in the United States?

NATIONAL STANDARDS CORRELATIONS:

NCSS Ic: (Culture) Explain and give examples of how language, literature, the arts, architecture, other artifacts, traditions, beliefs, values, and behaviors contribute to the development and transmission of culture.
NSH Era 10, Standard 2: Economic, social, and cultural developments in the contemporary United States

WEBSITES:

http://lcweb2.loc.gov/ammem/collections/robinson/
"Baseball and Jackie Robinson," The Library of Congress

http://www.oscars.org/mhl/sc/mcdaniel_105.html
"Hattie McDaniel Collection," Academy of Motion Picture Arts and Sciences

http://www.liu.edu/cwis/cwp/library/aaitsa.htm
"African-Americans in the Sports Arena," Long Island University

http://ncadi.samhsa.gov/seasonal/blackhistory/prominent.aspx
"Black History Month," U.S. Department of Health and Human Services and SAMHSA's National Clearinghouse for Alcohol & Drug Information

Affirmative Action and Busing

Affirmative action. In the Civil Rights Act of 1964, Congress required that the government make rules to end discrimination. No one was certain what this meant or how it should be done. It took five years before the Department of Labor required that businesses with government contracts have an "affirmative action" program. By 1972, the term was applied to college admissions and state and national government agencies as well as businesses. Affirmative action tries to give minorities and women an equal opportunity to get a job, an education, or a promotion. If a company or government agency has less than an average number of women or minorities in its workforce, it must draw up a plan to reach that number.

Debating the issues

The purpose is to give those who have always been at a disadvantage a chance to catch up. The law speaks of "goals," which many assumed to be "quotas." If 10 percent of the community were African-American and 51 percent were female, then the XYZ Company's workforce of 100 employees should have 10 African-Americans and 51 women employees. Restrictions having nothing to do with a person's ability to do the job must be removed.

The problem comes when those who do not get jobs feel that the hiring standards are lower for minorities than for them. This is called "reverse discrimination." After Allan Bakke learned that minority students who had lower grades and test scores than he had were admitted under a quota system, he took the University of California to court. The Supreme Court majority ruled in 1978 that the university could use race as part of admitting students, but its rigid quota violated Bakke's rights.

Busing. When courts ordered that schools be desegregated, many whites moved to the suburbs. In inner-city Detroit, for instance, the schools were 70 percent African-American, but in the suburbs, they were 80 percent white. There were few whites in the cities with whom African-Americans could integrate. In Boston, the federal judge ordered that African-American students be admitted to South High School, which was all-white.

Some African-American leaders favored busing students between the city and the suburbs to get a racial mix. In 1975, a district court ordered Louisville to bus students into Jefferson County. When violence occurred and 50 people were injured, the Kentucky National Guard was called in, and the judge ordered that armed guards ride on the buses. After that, tempers calmed.

When the Boston School Committee rejected court-ordered busing in 1975, saying that it created racial tension, the judge felt that the board was not cooperating with the law. He decided to place the schools under court control after African-Americans told him how they had been treated by their fellow students.

RESULTS: Affirmative action and busing both have many supporters and critics within and outside the African-American community. Supporters say these practices are necessary to give African-Americans an equal opportunity. Critics say they create more tension than advantage.

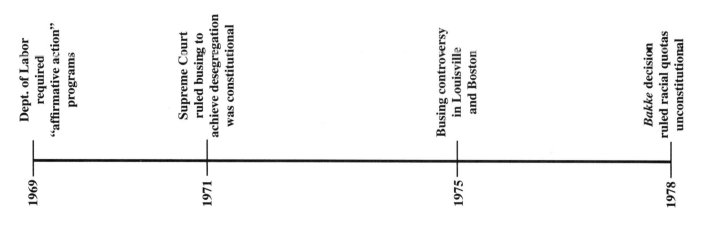

Name: _____ Date: _____

Affirmative Action and Busing: Reinforcement

Directions: Complete the following activities, essays, and challenges on your own paper.

ACTIVITIES:

1. Have a class discussion on what is the best way for African-Americans to catch up with whites on the job market.
2. If the class were a school board, what kinds of questions would people ask them about a court-ordered busing program?

ESSAYS:

1. Write in favor of or against busing to achieve integration.
2. Write in favor of or against affirmative action to achieve integration.
3. Do you think reverse discrimination is a problem? Why or why not?

CHALLENGES:

1. Who required that businesses with government contracts have an "affirmative action" program?
2. The purpose of affirmative action is to do what?
3. What term is used instead of "quotas"?
4. If a company does not have enough minority or women workers, what is it supposed to do?
5. What is "reverse discrimination"?
6. Who took a case of reverse discrimination to the Supreme Court?
7. What was a reason that court-ordered desegregation in big cities did not work as planned?
8. What border state city had trouble when it tried busing from the city to the county school systems?
9. What argument did the Boston School Committee give for opposing busing?
10. What did the federal judge do in Boston?

NATIONAL STANDARDS CORRELATIONS:

NCSS Xg: (Civic Ideals & Practices) Analyze the influence of diverse forms of public opinion on the development of public policy and decision-making.
NSH Era 10, Standard 2: Economic, social, and cultural developments in the contemporary United States

WEBSITES:

http://clinton2.nara.gov/WH/EOP/OP/html/aa/aa02.html
"Affirmative Action: History and Rationale," The U.S. National Archives and Records Administration

http://www.richmondhistorycenter.com/busing/busingTimeline.html
"On the Front Line of Integration: Memories of School Busing in Richmond, Virginia," Richmond History Center

http://www.constitutioncenter.org/timeline/html/cw12_12308.html
"Centuries of Citizenship: A Constitutional Timeline," National Constitution Center

http://www.pbs.org/wgbh/pages/frontline/shows/sats/race/summary.html
"Challenging Race-Sensitive Admissions Policies," Public Broadcasting Service

Colin Powell: Top General and Diplomat

Colin Powell

Colin Luther Powell was the first African-American to become the national security advisor, the chairman of the U.S. Joint Chiefs of Staff, and the secretary of state. He also became a national hero for his work during the Persian Gulf Crisis and War.

Powell was born in New York City on April 5, 1937. He was the son of Jamaican immigrants and grew up in the Harlem and South Bronx neighborhoods of New York City. He graduated from the City College of New York in 1958. While in college, he enrolled in the Reserve Officers Training Corps (ROTC). He then entered the army as a second lieutenant. He later earned his master's degree from George Washington University in Washington, D.C.

In 1962, Powell married Alma Johnson, and the couple had a son (Michael) in 1963, a daughter (Linda) in 1965, and another daughter (Annemarie) in 1971.

During the Vietnam War, Powell served two tours of duty. The first was from 1962 to 1963, and the second was from 1968 to 1969. By this time, he was a major. In 1973, he became a lieutenant colonel and was sent to command the First Battalion in Korea.

Powell held executive positions at the Pentagon and the White House during the administrations of seven presidents. He first worked in the White House in 1972 as a White House Fellow. In 1983, he became the military assistant to Secretary of Defense Caspar Weinberger. In 1987, Powell joined the staff of the National Security Council and was appointed the national security advisor by President Ronald Reagan later that year.

Just two years later, Powell became a four-star general, and President George H.W. Bush appointed him as chairman of the Joint Chiefs of Staff. The Joint Chiefs of Staff is an agency in the Department of Defense that advises the president on military policy. It has representatives from the army, navy, air force, and marines. The chairmanship is the highest military post in the United States.

Powell had the responsibility for the 1989 invasion of Panama. He was also in charge of the U.S. military operations against Iraq in the Persian Gulf War. These included both the Desert Shield and Desert Storm operations from August 1990 to March 1991.

Great Britain awarded Powell an honorary knighthood in 1993. That same year, he retired from the military. In 1995, he wrote his autobiography, *My American Journey*. Powell considered a run for the presidency in 1996 but withdrew his name as a candidate because he did not wish to have his family go through a presidential campaign. He then accepted the position of general chairman of the President's Summit for America's Freedom. The group's goal is to raise funds and enlist volunteers to help combat poverty and social problems in the United States.

In 2001, newly elected President George W. Bush appointed Powell as secretary of state. In this position, Powell worked closely with the president to develop foreign policy between the United States and the Middle East, Russia, and elsewhere. He was an important voice for the United States at the United Nations while making the case for the War on Terror and the invasion of Afghanistan and Iraq following the terrorist attacks on September 11, 2001.

Colin Powell resigned from the secretary of state's position in 2005 at the end of George W. Bush's first term.

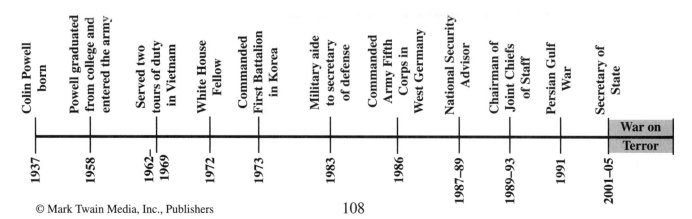

Name: _____ Date: _____

Colin Powell: Top General and Diplomat: Reinforcement

Directions: Complete the following activities, essays, and challenges on your own paper.

ACTIVITIES:

1. Do some research and make a list of the presidents for whom Colin Powell has worked in executive positions in either the Pentagon or the White House.
2. Many people think Colin Powell would make a good president. Make a campaign poster that highlights his achievements and his qualifications for the office.

ESSAYS:

1. What are some of the changes that have taken place in the military in regard to race relations from the time Colin Powell was born to today?
2. Do you think Colin Powell would make a good president? Why or why not?
3. Do you think Colin Powell could be elected president? Why or why not?

CHALLENGES:

1. From where did Colin Powell's parents come?
2. What does ROTC stand for?
3. During what war did Powell serve two tours of duty?
4. Where did Powell command the First Battalion?
5. Who appointed Powell to be the national security advisor?
6. What is the highest military post in the United States?
7. The Persian Gulf War included what two military operations?
8. Which president appointed Powell to be chairman of the Joint Chiefs of Staff?
9. Powell was secretary of state during which president's first term?
10. As secretary of state, to which important international group did Powell speak about the War on Terror?

NATIONAL STANDARDS CORRELATIONS:

NCSS Xf: (Civic Ideals & Practices) Identify and explain the roles of formal and informal political actors in influencing and shaping public policy and decision-making.
NSH Era 10, Standard 2: Economic, social, and cultural developments in the contemporary United States

WEBSITES:

http://www.whitehouse.gov/government/powell-bio.html
"Secretary of State Colin L. Powell," The White House

http://americanhistory.si.edu/militaryhistory/collection/object.asp?ID=165
"Colin Powell's Battle Dress Uniform," Smithsonian Institute

Condoleezza Rice: Political Powerhouse

Condoleezza Rice

In a recent survey by Forbes magazine, Condoleezza Rice was named the most powerful woman in the world. This could be quite true, since as the secretary of state, Rice is the highest-ranking diplomat representing the United States in its dealings with other nations. Rice was appointed the secretary of state in January 2005 by President George W. Bush as he began his second term.

This may seem unlikely for a girl born in Birmingham, Alabama, on November 14, 1954, during the height of segregation and racial tension. But due to her strong family (her father was a Presbyterian minister, teacher, coach, and guidance counselor, and her mother was a high school music and science teacher) who always stressed education, achievement, and faith, she always felt she could accomplish whatever she put her mind to. Her mother, who was a pianist and organist, named her Condoleezza from the musical term *con dolcezza,* which means to play "with sweetness." She grew up in the tight-knit African-American community of Titusville in Birmingham, where the parents tried to shield their children from the violence of the Civil Rights movement. However, the racism and violence of those years was impossible to ignore. Condoleezza missed many days of school in 1963 because of bomb threats at her segregated school. In September 1963, she attended the funeral for four young girls killed in the bombing of the Sixteenth Street Baptist Church. The youngest girl killed had been one of Condoleezza's friends.

On one of the family's many educational trips, they visited Washington, D.C., and stopped to view the White House. After staring quietly at the great building, Condoleezza turned to her father and said, "Daddy, I'm barred out of there now because of the color of my skin. But one day, I'll be in that house." Condoleezza Rice first came to work at the White House from 1989 to 1991 during the administration of President George H.W. Bush as his top advisor on the Soviet Union.

After spending her childhood and teenage years training to be a concert pianist, Rice became interested in international relations and government while at the University of Denver. Her specialty was the Soviet Union, and she learned to speak Russian fluently. She graduated in 1974, received her M.A. in government from Notre Dame University in 1975, and received her Ph.D. in international studies from the University of Denver in 1981. She taught political science at Stanford University and became the provost of the university in 1993. In this post, she was responsible for the university's budget and academic policies, second only to the president of the university. She was the youngest person (age 38), the first African-American, and the first woman to hold the position.

While working closely with the senior Bush on a book about the major global events that had occurred during his administration, Rice became acquainted with the rest of the Bush family, even spending some vacations with them. She first met George W. Bush when he was governor of Texas. The two became friends, and he often discussed foreign relations with her. When Bush decided to run for president, Rice was brought into the campaign as his chief advisor on foreign policy. Rice was also an important symbol of the Bush commitment to women and minorities.

The newly elected President Bush appointed Rice to be the national security advisor, and she took over that position in January 2001. The national security advisor consolidates the views of the secretary of state, the secretary of defense, and other members of the National Security Council and brings them to the president. Rice was an important part of the team that developed strategy for dealing with terrorists and homeland security during the War on Terror, after the terrorist attacks on September 11, 2001.

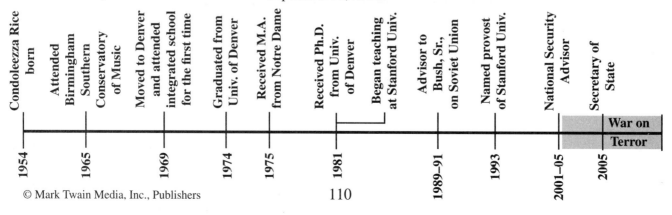

Name: _____ Date: _____

Condoleezza Rice: Political Powerhouse: Reinforcement

Directions: Complete the following activities, essays, and challenges on your own paper.

ACTIVITIES:

1. Condoleezza Rice is an accomplished pianist and had even thought of pursuing that as her career. List some other examples of people in politics or business who are also musicians or artists.
2. Imagine that you are a reporter who has an opportunity to interview Condoleezza Rice. Think of five questions you would like to ask her, and research to find out what her answers might be.

ESSAYS:

1. Many people think Condoleezza Rice would make a good president. Do you agree? Why or why not?
2. What are some of the duties of the secretary of state?
3. Do you think the Forbes magazine survey was right to call Condoleezza Rice the most powerful woman in the world?

CHALLENGES:

1. To what position was Condoleezza Rice appointed in January 2005?
2. Who appointed Rice as his national security advisor?
3. Where was Rice born?
4. Where did her mother get the idea for her first name?
5. Why were there bombings in Rice's hometown?
6. Where did Rice first become interested in international relations and government?
7. Rice was George H.W. Bush's top advisor on what country?
8. When Rice first met George W. Bush, what was his title?
9. In addition to advising Bush on foreign policy, why was Rice good for the campaign?
10. Rice was an important member of the team that developed the strategy for which war?

NATIONAL STANDARDS CORRELATIONS:

NCSS Xf: (Civic Ideals & Practices) Identify and explain the roles of formal and informal political actors in influencing and shaping public policy and decision-making.
NSH Era 10, Standard 2: Economic, social, and cultural developments in the contemporary United States

WEBSITES:

http://www.whitehouse.gov/nsc/ricebio.html
"Biography of Dr. Condoleezza Rice, National Security Advisor," The White House

http://www.state.gov/secretary/
"Secretary of State: Condoleezza Rice," U.S. Department of State

Answer Keys

A New Market for the Slave Trade (page 5)

1. The Bantu arrived around 1000 B.C.
2. The Bantu bought salt and copper and sold ivory, gold, and slaves.
3. There were 264 Sudanese languages and 182 Bantu languages.
4. The first kingdom was Ghana, ruled by the Soninke family.
5. Mali was south and east of Ghana; its ruler was Mansa Musa.
6. The center of learning was Timbuktu.
7. Two important Songhai rulers were Sonni Ali and Askia Mohammed Ture.
8. The ruler of Benin was called the Oba, who ruled through his relatives
9. The captain was from Portugal; he wanted to trade in ivory, gold, and slaves.
10. Portugal, England, and Holland were involved in the slave trade.

Las Casas in the West Indies (page 7)

1. An *encomienda* was an estate where work was done by Native Americans.
2. Las Casas was a priest.
3. Antonio de Montesinos was a priest who attacked the *encomiendas* on Santo Domingo.
4. The Spanish thought of the natives as savages: pagan, naked, lazy, idol worshipers.
5. Natives refused the king's offer because the instructions were in languages they did not understand.
6. Las Casas thought they could tolerate the work and heat better than the Native Americans who were being wiped out.
7. A permit to import slaves was an *asiento*.
8. Factories were holding areas for slaves.
9. Estevanico (Little Stephen) was a scout for Marcos.
10. *Quilombos* were colonies in Brazil run by escaped slaves; the most famous was Palmarea, which lasted 67 years.

Slaves in the American Colonies (page 9)

1. Rome used slaves as police and ship captains.
2. Persons in the underclass were serfs, peasants, villeins, and slaves.
3. Africans used slaves as soldiers, caravan workers, and royal officials.
4. Caboceer was the term used for agents appointed by African kings to deal with slave traders.

5. Henry VIII ordered the Irish's obedience.
6. The London Company sent 100 poor children as "bound apprentices."
7. The first Africans were purchased from the Dutch.
8. The 20 Africans were "bound servants."
9. South Carolina feared that too many slaves would cause the price to fall.
10. Oglethorpe wanted the land reserved for English debtors.

The Middle Passage (page 11)

1. The goods carried were cloth, guns, or rum.
2. Slaves were carried in the 'tween decks section—between the deck above and the hold below.
3. Slave space was 16 inches wide; 5.5 feet long; and 3 feet, 10 inches high.
4. The portholes were closed to keep slaves from jumping overboard.
5. Yellow fever, dysentery, and malaria were some of the diseases.
6. Slaves were hungry, scared, and unable to communicate because they all spoke different languages.
7. Food and water were provided so the slaves would bring a better price.
8. To prevent them from starving, a heated funnel was pressed against their lips and they were forced to eat.
9. There were 55 documented slave revolts; there was mention of hundreds of others.
10. Slaves on the *Perfect* ran it ashore and then looted and burned it.

Slavery as a Social and Legal System (page 13)

1. People became indentured servants to pay for their transportation to America.
2. Apprentices were young people who were orphans or with poor parents and who were given to a tradesman to be trained.
3. 10,000 convicts were sent to Maryland in a 20-year period.
4. The Duke of York, the brother of the king, led the Company of Royal Adventurers.
5. West Indian planters sold slaves because crop production was dropping.
6. Slave marriages were approved because they produced workers to replace themselves.
7. A slave who became a Christian was still a slave.
8. Children inherited their mother's status.

9. Georgia limit: no more than seven African-Americans could be gathered unless a white person was present.

10. A slave could not testify against a white person in New York.

Slavery in the American Revolution (page 15)

1. The African slave trade was argued against in "Summary View."

2. The inalienable rights are life, liberty, and pursuit of happiness.

3. Salem Poor distinguished himself at Bunker Hill (Breed's Hill).

4. Lord Dunmore encouraged Virginian African-Americans to join the English cause.

5. New York gave freedom to any slave serving three years in the militia.

6. The states refusing to enlist African-Americans were South Carolina and Georgia.

7. The states with largest numbers of African-American volunteers were Massachusetts and Rhode Island.

8. The most famous African-American sailor was James Forten.

9. John Jay, Ben Franklin, and Benjamin Rush spoke out against slavery.

10. Northern states abolished slavery; Southern states made it easier to free slaves.

Constitutional Compromises on Slavery (page 17)

1. The problems worrying leaders in 1787 were foreign intrigue, state rivalries, and mobs.

2. Slavery seemed minor because of so many other major issues.

3. The Northwest Ordinance barred slavery in territories north of the Ohio River.

4. Fugitive slaves fleeing to the Northwest Territories had to be returned.

5. The South did not want slaves to be counted if a poll (head) tax was levied.

6. The North did not want to count slaves when it came to state representation in Congress.

7. Slaves were to be counted as 3/5 of a person for both taxation and representation.

8. The states opposing an end to African slave trade were South Carolina and Georgia.

9. The Convention agreed to let slave trade continue for another 20 years (1807).

10. Fugitive slaves were to be returned to their masters.

Some African-Americans Defy Stereotypes (page 19)

1. Jefferson said that slaves were better off than English workers.

2. Aristotle said that there was a slave class who was incapable of thinking for themselves, so they needed someone to tell them what to do.

3. Alexis de Tocqueville believed the race factor made American slavery different.

4. Vassa angered his master by asking to buy his freedom; he was then sold in the West Indies.

5. In Jamaica, Vassa managed a sugar plantation.

6. Wheatley was able to read the Bible 16 months after her arrival.

7. Wheatley excelled at poetry.

8. Wheatley was praised by George Washington.

9. Banneker was a biologist, astronomer, and engineer.

10. Banneker worked with L'Enfant on the layout of Washington, D.C.

The Cotton Gin and Slavery (page 21)

1. It was easy for the owner to claim a runaway slave under the Fugitive Slave Act of 1793.

2. Tobacco was the main crop before cotton to use slaves.

3. Rice was limited to the coastal regions of Georgia and South Carolina.

4. Sea island and upland cotton were the two main varieties.

5. Gin was an abbreviation for "engine."

6. Samuel Slater built the first U.S. cotton mill.

7. Both came in 1793.

8. Cotton was grown from Georgia to Mississippi. (Later, the area expanded into parts of Louisiana and Texas.)

9. Cotton's main markets were England and the North.

10. Over half of the slaves were involved in cotton production.

Slaves Find Power in Religion (page 23)

1. Slaves found hope and power in religion.

2. Slaves sat in the balcony or in the back of white churches.

3. The topics were to obey their masters, not to steal, morality, or church doctrine.

4. A slave preacher could be punished for getting out of line.

5. Slave music was rhythmic: they clapped their hands, kept time with their feet, and tossed their heads.

6. The most common type of song was the spiritual.

7. Substitute "master" for "pharaoh."

8. Substitute "North" for "Canaan."

9. The day of jubilee was the day they would be freed.

10. God would reward them in heaven.

Northern African-Americans Form Separate Churches (page 25)

1. African-Americans sat in corners, in balconies, or in back pews.
2. Allen was trained by a traveling evangelist.
3. The Free African Society helped widows and orphans, provided burial space, and supported the Pennsylvania Abolition Society.
4. Jones was the minister of the St. Thomas Protestant Episcopal Church with the first African-American congregation.
5. Allen was Methodist.
6. Allen formed the African Methodist Episcopal church (AME) and was bishop.
7. Catholics did not segregate.
8. At some Quaker meetings, African-Americans were treated as equals, while at others, African-Americans were segregated or refused membership.
9. DeGrasse was asked to withdraw as a student.
10. The Union Theological Seminary put up no barriers.

African-Americans Oppose Colonization (page 27)

1. Philadelphia leaders mobilizing African-Americans were James Forten, Richard Allen, Absalom Jones.
2. Slaves were used by General Andrew Jackson at New Orleans.
3. Cuffe spent $4,000 to transport 38 African-Americans to Africa.
4. The purpose of the ACS was to return African-Americans to Africa.
5. Some early ACS members were Francis Scott Key, Henry Clay, John Randolph, and James Monroe.
6. The first were returned in 1820; many died of malaria.
7. Liberia developed because of the ACS.
8. The capital was Monrovia, named after President Monroe.
9. African-Americans felt that they were Americans, not Africans.
10. They said the motive was to send free African-Americans to Africa so they could keep other African-Americans as slaves.

The Missouri Compromise (page 29)

1. The president during the Era of Good Feelings was James Monroe.
2. Issues splitting the Republicans were tariffs, internal improvements, and slavery.
3. The French and Spanish brought slaves into Missouri before 1804.
4. James Tallmadge proposed that no more slaves be brought into Missouri.
5. The most supportive party was the Federalists.
6. The Tallmadge Amendment was removed by the Senate.
7. The Missouri Compromise allowed slavery south of 36°30′ in the Louisiana Purchase.
8. The other state was Maine.
9. Missouri wanted to block free African-Americans from entering the state.
10. Clay's compromise: Missouri could not bar citizens of other states from entering. He did not define if free African-Americans were citizens.

Slaves Make a Life for Themselves (page 31)

1. The problem was that by the time interviews were conducted, most former slaves had died, and those remaining were very old.
2. Former slaves who wrote of their experiences were Frederick Douglass and William Wells Brown.
3. Thomas Jefferson supplied brick cottages.
4. African-American supervisors were called drivers.
5. White supervisors were called overseers.
6. The ways in which slaves were used as property were that they could be bought, sold, lent, or rented out. (When their master died, they were also part of the estate.)
7. Some of the ways in which a slave made money were by selling food from his garden or working on holidays.
8. Popular musical instruments were banjos, drums, and fiddles.
9. Some of the ways in which a young man showed a girl he was interested in her: impress her, give her presents, or win her mother's approval.
10. Sometimes a couple jumped over a broomstick together.

Slaves Rebel in Different Ways (page 33)

1. Some of the quiet rebellions were to loaf, pretend to be sick, break tools, steal, and leave a gate open.
2. If slaves could read and write, they would be able to forge passes, read abolitionist materials, and begin to think for themselves.
3. Vesey won enough money in a lottery to buy his freedom.
4. The revolt was in Charleston, S.C.
5. Turner saw signs in the heavens and in leaves.
6. About 60 whites were killed.
7. Whites were concerned because they did not know where Nat Turner was.
8. Turner and the other leaders were executed.

9. Turner was said to have read *The Liberator*.
10. The South feared Northern agitators as well.

The Abolition Movement (page 35)
1. Douglass read *The Liberator*.
2. Douglass gave his first speech at an anti-slavery convention at Nantucket, Massachusetts.
3. Walker suggested that slaves should use violence to revolt.
4. The "lightning rod" was William Lloyd Garrison.
5. Douglass owned and edited the *North Star*.
6. Brown worked with Elijah Lovejoy.
7. Sarah and Angelina Grimke were a sister team who fought slavery.
8. Two African-American women, Sojourner Truth and Harriet Tubman, were active abolitionists.
9. Strong voices supporting the anti-slavery cause were Joshua Giddings and John Q. Adams.
10. "Old Man Eloquent" was John Q. Adams.

Slavery Debates in Congress (page 37)
1. The quote was from William Lloyd Garrison.
2. The editor was Elijah Lovejoy.
3. The gag rule prevented any petition about slavery from being considered.
4. John Quincy Adams led the fight against the gag rule.
5. Texas waited 9 years.
6. The Wilmot Proviso barred slavery from any territory taken from Mexico.
7. The South opposed California because there would be more free states than slave states in the Union.
8. The Compromise of 1850 was written by Henry Clay and Stephen Douglas.
9. Popular sovereignty allowed people in a territory to choose whether or not to allow slavery.
10. The South was happiest over the strong Fugitive Slave Act.

The Underground Railroad (page 39)
1. Freedom papers showed that they were legally free.
2. The slave captured in Boston was Anthony Burns.
3. Butternuts were southern-born farmers living north of the Ohio River.
4. Slaves were suspicious because some whites would capture and sell them as slaves.
5. The North Star helped runaways to find the right direction in the dark.
6. African-Americans involved were likely to be killed.
7. Mason helped 1,300 slaves to escape.
8. Tubman made 19 trips and rescued 300 slaves.

9. It is estimated that 100,000 escaped.
10. It is estimated that there were 3,200 agents.

Uncle Tom vs. Blackface Minstrels (page 41)
1. The full title was *Uncle Tom's Cabin, or Life Among the Lowly*.
2. Stowe's experience with slavery: She had been a guest of a Kentucky plantation owner; she hid runaway slaves in her house.
3. Simon Legree was the cruel overseer.
4. The number of copies that were sold in America was 300,000.
5. The number of copies that were sold in England was 1.5 million.
6. Abraham Lincoln said that she had started the war.
7. Minstrels dressed in ridiculous costumes and wore black makeup.
8. Immigrants enjoyed the minstrels.
9. Stephen Foster wrote for minstrel shows.
10. The most famous were the Christy's Minstrels.

The Battle Over Kansas (page 43)
1. The United States wanted to use it to build a railroad to California.
2. The chairman was Stephen Douglas.
3. Douglas suggested the Kansas and Nebraska Territories.
4. The territorial government needed to survey and sell land and protect the railroad.
5. Pierce leaned toward the southern position.
6. The two legislatures were Lecompton (pro-slave) and Topeka (anti-slavery).
7. A pro-southern politician from the North was called a doughface.
8. A person opposing slavery in the territories was called a free soiler.
9. The town attacked was Lawrence, Kansas.
10. The person attacked was Charles Sumner.

Courts, Debates, and Attacks (page 45)
1. Scott thought he should be freed because he had lived in free areas.
2. The majority decision was handed down by Roger Taney.
3. The points made were that African-Americans were not citizens and the Missouri Compromise was unconstitutional.
4. Frederick Douglass hoped the decision would raise the "National Conscience" of white public opinion.
5. Stephen Douglas's opponent was Abraham Lincoln.
6. Douglas stated that people in the territory could stop

slavery by not protecting slave property.

7. Douglas was reelected.

8. Brown picked Harpers Ferry because there was a federal arsenal there.

9. Brown planned to build an army of escaped slaves as he moved down the Appalachians.

10. Brown was captured, tried, and executed.

African-Americans Agitate for Freedom (page 47)

1. The number of Confederate states was 11.

2. The number of slave states in the Union was 4.

3. The groups who were opposed to freeing slaves were Democrats and poor immigrants.

4. Abraham Lincoln called slavery an "unqualified evil."

5. Three African-Americans who were critical of Lincoln's go-slow policy were Tubman, Pennington, and Douglass.

6. The nickname for runaways was "contrabands."

7. Frémont wanted to free the slaves of Confederate sympathizers.

8. Crittenden-Johnson freed no slaves.

9. The second Confiscation Act freed slaves escaping to Union lines.

10. The Emancipation Proclamation freed slaves in Confederate hands as of January 1, 1863.

African-Americans Fight for Freedom (page 49)

1. Most did not leave until the Union army was nearby.

2. Patrick Cleburne first suggested that the Confederacy use African-American troops.

3. Lorenzo Thomas organized African-American troops in the Mississippi Valley.

4. Two officers who commanded African-American regiments were Thomas Higginson and Robert Shaw.

5. The pay for white soldiers (including clothing) was $16.50; African-Americans only received $10.

6. The pay was equalized in 1864.

7. It was called the Ft. Pillow "massacre" because the African-Americans who were trying to surrender were shot.

8. The 54th Massachusetts lost 247 out of 600 men.

9. The South was hurt by declining African-Americans' help in the war effort.

10. They received special respect because of a strong desire to prove themselves in combat.

The Road to Freedom (page 51)

1. The day of jubilee was the day when freedom was to come.

2. Some of the problems facing farmers were destroyed barns and a shortage of horses, mules, plows, and harnesses.

3. Andrew Johnson replaced Lincoln.

4. Those who were allowed to vote were whites who had signed a loyalty oath.

5. Conventions could be formed only after enough whites had signed oaths.

6. White thugs usually started race riots.

7. Black Codes replaced slave codes.

8. African-Americans could only testify in cases involving other African-Americans.

9. In the Black Codes, the parts limiting economic activity: African-Americans had to live up to contracts; they couldn't enter certain trades; and they were charged fines for vagrancy.

10. If they were unemployed, they could be rented out by the sheriff to pay the fine.

Reconstruction (page 53)

1. The radical Republican leaders were Thaddeus Stevens and Charles Sumner.

2. The veto of the Freedmen's Bureau and the Civil Rights bills caused opinions to change.

3. Two provisions of the Reconstruction Act were a military government for the South and a new loyalty oath.

4. Northern allies were called carpetbaggers.

5. Southern allies were called scalawags.

6. Two African-Americans were elected to the Senate; twenty were elected to the House.

7. Schools received strong support.

8. Some important expenditures were for schools, roads, and railroads.

9. The most famous terrorist group of the time was the Ku Klux Klan.

10. Union Leaguers, Yankee schoolteachers, Freedmen's Bureau agents, carpetbaggers, and scalawags were targeted.

From Slavery to Sharecropping (page 55)

1. The promise of 40 acres and a mule was music to the ears of freedmen.

2. Sherman set aside land on offshore islands.

3. Croppers could appeal to the Freedmen's Bureau courts.

4. African-Americans didn't like gang labor because it was too much like slavery.

5. The sharecropper and the landowner (usually) split 50–50.

6. The cropper had to pay off his debts before he received any money.

7. After paying cash, the tenant usually gave the landowner one-third of the crop.
8. The farmer signed a lien with the merchant.
9. If his debts were not paid, he could not leave.
10. B.T. Washington said that it was as bad as slavery.

Cowboys, Exodusters, and Soldiers (page 57)

1. Two African-American explorers were Estevanico and York.
2. Two African-American fur traders were Jean DeSable and James Beckwourth.
3. There were about 5,000 African-American cowboys.
4. Bill Pickett's sport was bulldogging.
5. Kansas offered transportation, land, and the first year's supplies.
6. Two exodus boosters were Benjamin "Pap" Singleton and Henry Adams.
7. African-American cavalry regiments were the 9th and 10th regiments; African-American infantry regiments were the 24th and 25th regiments.
8. They were called "buffalo soldiers" by the Cheyenne because of their dark, kinky hair.
9. Four scouts received the medal of honor.
10. Three buffalo soldier officers were Henry Flipper, Ben Grierson, and John J. Pershing.

African-Americans Head North (page 59)

1. The system that rented out convicts was called convict leasing.
2. Officials sold the crops the prisoners produced and kept the money from their food allowance.
3. There were 3,500 lynchings during those years.
4. African-Americans were tied to the South by family, friendships, and church.
5. Chicago increased by 35,000.
6. Rent was up because the area open to African-Americans was limited, and more were arriving.
7. Respectable African-Americans were unhappy because they could not control their neighborhoods.
8. The African-American area of Chicago was called the South Side; the African-American area of New York was called Harlem.
9. Important social institutions were church, fraternal orders, and charitable groups.
10. The least discriminatory union was the Knights of Labor.

Booker T. Washington (page 61)

1. Alabama appropriated $2,000.
2. Washington was trained at the Hampton Institute.
3. Washington was recommended by O.K. Armstrong.

4. Washington believed all students should work.
5. Men learned bricklaying, carpentry, blacksmithing, and farming.
6. Women learned cooking, sewing, and housekeeping.
7. The program to help the farmers was the Tuskegee Agricultural Experiment Station.
8. George Washington Carver was the famous scientist who taught at Tuskegee.
9. Carver held field demonstrations and traveled there in a two-horse vehicle donated by a New York philanthropist.
10. Rosenwald funded 5,000 African-American schools in rural areas.

The Disfranchising of African-Americans (page 63)

1. The Farmers' Alliance movement developed to form the Populist party.
2. The Populist who was trying to win African-American support was Tom Watson.
3. Two populists who opposed the African-American vote were Ben Tillman and J.K. Vardaman.
4. The Fifteenth Amendment stood in the way of disfranchisement.
5. Republicans were pulling away from African-Americans to win white voters.
6. Literacy tests asked more difficult questions of African-Americans than of whites.
7. The South said that the Blair Bill was an attack on literacy tests (which it was).
8. The real reason for the poll tax was to keep African-Americans and poor whites from voting.
9. When the Democratic Party became a club, it could keep African-Americans out.
10. The author of the Force Bill was Henry Cabot Lodge; it failed to pass because the Senate had adjourned.

"Separate but Equal" (page 65)

1. The other name for segregation was Jim Crow laws.
2. *Civil Rights Cases* stated that the Fourteenth Amendment protected only against state, and not private, actions.
3. African-American schools received poor equipment and less tax support; their teachers were paid less.
4. State facilities that were segregated were for the insane, blind, deaf, and imprisoned.
5. Washington feared that African-Americans might lose their jobs to immigrants.
6. His speech did not demand social equality.
7. His speech pleased the governor and President Cleveland.

8. W.E.B. DuBois was critical; he said that Washington had surrendered to racism.
9. Plessy boarded a railroad car that was reserved for whites.
10. The Supreme Court said that segregation did not mean racial inferiority.

Founding the NAACP (page 67)
1. Statesboro rioters were never punished.
2. The group that was formed as a result of the Atlanta riot was the Atlanta Civic League.
3. The first African-American to earn a Ph.D. was W.E.B. DuBois.
4. The publisher of *The Guardian* was William Trotter.
5. The group they started was called the Niagara Movement.
6. The Movement demanded the right to vote for African-American men, the enforcing of the Constitution, and education for their children.
7. The duties listed were to vote, work, obey the law, be clean and orderly, send their children to school, and to have self-respect.
8. The Springfield riot was different because it was in Lincoln's hometown.
9. The names of the three leaders were Walling, Ovington, and Moskowitz.
10. The name of the NAACP magazine was *The Crisis.*

The Urban League (page 69)
1. African-Americans were also coming from the West Indies, South Africa, and South America.
2. Haynes was interested in the social and economic conditions of African-Americans in the city.
3. The Urban League was formed in 1911.
4. The areas that were focused on were housing, health, sanitation, recreation, self-improvement, and job assistance.
5. Migrants were met at the train, directed to housing and jobs, and given information about city living.
6. The church bought ten apartment houses and rented them to African-Americans.
7. The major concerns of the YMCA and YWCA were social, recreational, and educational opportunities.
8. After their pledge of $50,000, African-Americans raised $65,000 in three weeks.
9. Rosenwald offered a $25,000 donation to any African-American community raising the other $25,000.
10. The fraternal orders that were important to African-Americans were the Masons, Odd Fellows, and Knights of Pythias.

African-Americans in World War I (page 71)
1. African-Americans were angry because Wilson segregated the restrooms and eating facilities in government buildings.
2. Job opportunities arose because of the war and a sudden drop in immigration.
3. 25,000 African-Americans were in the army and militia at the beginning.
4. African-Americans who were drafted numbered 367,000.
5. General Leonard Wood established African-American officers' training camps.
6. His confidential advisor was Emmet Scott, former secretary to Booker T. Washington.
7. Training for the 92nd was unusual because it was done at seven different camps.
8. Most African-American units worked at unloading ships or served in labor battalions.
9. The unit known as the "Hell Fighters" was the 369th Infantry.
10. The unit fighting in the last battle was the 370th Infantry.

Postwar America (page 73)
1. During the Red Scare, radical immigrants were chased out.
2. The number of riots in 1919 was 25.
3. The Chicago riot lasted 13 days, and 40 were killed.
4. Omaha, Nebraska, had a riot.
5. The group formed was named the Commission on Interracial Cooperation (CIC).
6. The movie, *Birth of a Nation,* glorified the Klan.
7. William Simmons was responsible for reorganizing the Klan.
8. Indiana and Oregon had a large membership.
9. Other targets of the Klan were Catholics, Jews, immigrants, and prohibition violators.
10. The Klan opposed Al Smith.

Marcus Garvey and Racial Pride (page 75)
1. The group Garvey formed was the Jamaica Improvement Association.
2. Garvey admired Booker T. Washington.
3. Garvey thought that African-Americans should stop asking for racial equality.
4. UNIA was an acronym for the United Negro Improvement Association.
5. His steamship company was the Black Star Line.
6. The three colors of his flag were red, black, green.
7. African-Americans were trying to look like whites by straightening their hair and bleaching their skin.

8. W.E.B. DuBois was a critic of Garvey.
9. Garvey was found guilty of mail fraud in the sale of Black Star Line stock.
10. Garvey served two years in federal prison and was deported to Jamaica.

Ragtime, Jazz, and Blues (page 77)

1. Four centers were New York, New Orleans, Memphis, and St. Louis.
2. Two early music forms were spiritual and work songs.
3. Instruments that were used had formerly been Civil War military band instruments.
4. Their main motive was enjoyment.
5. The piano was usually used for ragtime.
6. The most important ragtime musician was Scott Joplin.
7. The two most famous ragtime songs were "The Entertainer" and "The Maple Leaf Rag."
8. The "Father of the Blues" was W.C. Handy.
9. Two famous blues songs were "Memphis Blues" and "St. Louis Blues."
10. The two most famous jazz band directors were Duke Ellington and Count Basie.

The New Deal (page 79)

1. DePriest's distinction: He was the first African-American to serve in Congress in the twentieth century.
2. The Supreme Court nominee defeated was John Parker.
3. The Hoover victory caused some Republicans to want to appeal to southern whites at the expense of African-Americans.
4. DePriest was defeated in 1934 by Arthur Miller, an African-American Democrat.
5. A prominent New Dealer was Harold Ickes.
6. FDR's African-American advisors were called the "Black Cabinet" or the "Black Brain Trust."
7. The agency affecting African-American industrial employment was the National Recovery Act (NRA).
8. The program that resulted in forcing African-American sharecroppers out was the Agricultural Adjustment Act (AAA).
9. The Civilian Conservation Corps (CCC) employed young African-American men in conservation.
10. The Works Progress Administration (WPA) and the Public Works Administration (PWA) hired African-Americans for projects and built buildings and playgrounds used by African-Americans.

Jobs Created by World War II (page 81)

1. The United Mine Workers (UMW) had always been open to African-Americans.
2. The Congress of Industrial Organizations (CIO) had recruited African-Americans from the beginning.
3. Hitler would not honor Jesse Owens as an Olympic medalist.
4. Max Schmeling boxed Joe Louis twice.
5. The initials were NDAC and OPM.
6. The union organized by Randolph was the Brotherhood of Sleeping Car Porters.
7. Randolph called off the march on Washington.
8. Roosevelt ordered an end to discrimination in government and defense industries.
9. The purpose of 8802 was that there would be no discrimination in defense plants because of "race, creed, color, or national origin."
10. The Committee on Fair Employment Practices investigated complaints.

African-Americans Fight in World War II (page 83)

1. There were 5,000.
2. Their first reaction was to pass over African-Americans.
3. The first African-American general was B.O. Davis.
4. The number sent overseas was 500,000.
5. The number of African-American WACs was 4,000.
6. African-American pilots were trained at Tuskegee.
7. The marines' experiment was successful.
8. Two units were the 761st Tank and the 614th Tank Destroyer battalions.
9. They were angry because POWs were being served, and African-Americans were not allowed to enter the restaurant.
10. A major wartime race riot occurred in Detroit.

Truman Stands Up for Equality (page 85)

1. The author was Gunnar Myrdal.
2. Myrdal believed that Americans were torn within themselves over the issue.
3. Truman had clashed with the KKK in the 1920s.
4. The Civil Rights Commission recommended that segregation be eliminated.
5. They recommended to end discrimination in higher education and to end segregation in the armed forces.
6. Southern Democrats were angry.
7. After the civil rights plank was adopted, southern Democrats walked out.
8. The name given to them was Dixiecrats.

9. The general who wanted integration was Matthew Ridgeway.
10. Federal employees were to be hired without discrimination based on race.

The Landmark *Brown* Decision (page 87)

1. There were 21 states with segregation laws.
2. Restrictive covenants were agreements not to sell homes to African-Americans.
3. The guilty verdicts were overturned because due process had been denied.
4. African-Americans weren't admitted into southern law schools.
5. Thurgood Marshall was one of the best.
6. The NAACP attacked law school treatment of African-Americans.
7. The three states were Missouri, Texas, and Oklahoma.
8. The *Brown* decision resulted in a 9–0 vote.
9. It said that "in the field of public education the doctrine of 'separate but equal' has no place. Separate educational facilities are inherently unequal."
10. Desegregation was to move forward "with all deliberate speed."

Moving to the Front of the Bus (page 89)

1. The "Southern Manifesto" was a promise to use all lawful means to protect segregation.
2. Mrs. Parks' "crime" was that she refused to give up her seat on the bus to a white man.
3. The Montgomery Improvement Association led the boycott.
4. The leader was Martin Luther King, Jr.
5. At that time, he was minister of the Dexter Street Baptist Church.
6. Carpooling was developed.
7. The writers were Henry David Thoreau and Mohandas Gandhi.
8. They would do nothing to provoke white revenge.
9. The leaders were charged with engaging in an unlawful boycott.
10. The boycott ended on December 20, 1956; Dr. King rode a bus.

Desegregating Little Rock Central High (page 91)

1. U.S. district courts worked with school boards.
2. The governor was Orval Faubus.
3. Eisenhower believed that laws don't change people's hearts.
4. After he was overruled, Faubus withdrew the National Guard.
5. President Eisenhower vowed this.

6. He federalized the Arkansas National Guard and sent in troops.
7. The terms were to comply with the court order and maintain a peaceable situation.
8. Faubus closed the schools and then formed a private corporation to run them.
9. The approach was rejected by the Court of Appeals.
10. CROSS was an acronym for the Committee to Retain Our Segregated Schools.

The Civil Rights Movement (page 93)

1. King's organization was the SCLC.
2. The first lunch counter demonstration was in Greensboro, North Carolina.
3. The SNCC was the movement formed in 1960.
4. The Congress Of Racial Equality (CORE) worked to end bus segregation.
5. The riders were called Freedom Riders.
6. Martin Luther King, Jr., wrote the letter.
7. Evers was the field secretary of the Mississippi NAACP.
8. The quote was by John F. Kennedy.
9. The march occurred in August 1963; over 200,000 people participated.
10. The speech was given by Martin Luther King, Jr.

Radical Movements (page 95)

1. Critics thought King's approach was too slow and too devoted to winning white approval.
2. The SNCC changed its membership policy by removing whites.
3. Stokely Carmichael first coined the term, "Black Power."
4. *De facto* meant segregation in reality.
5. Richard Wright wrote *Native Son*.
6. Ralph Ellison wrote *Invisible Man*.
7. They did not used tobacco or alcohol.
8. Two famous converts were Cassius Clay (Muhammad Ali) and Malcolm Little (Malcolm X).
9. Some types of businesses run by Black Muslims were department stores, restaurants, and farms.
10. Malcolm X founded the Organization of Afro-American Unity.

The Civil and Voting Rights Acts (page 97)

1. The Civil Rights Act of 1957 gave the attorney-general the power.
2. James Meredith attended the University of Mississippi.
3. Governor George Wallace tried to prevent African-Americans from attending.

4. The Civil Rights Act of 1964 required that restaurants allow service to be offered to African-Americans.

5. Literacy tests and registration at odd hours of the day and night were some of the registrars' tactics.

6. Selma, Alabama, became its focus.

7. The distance was 54 miles.

8. About 600 went on the march; they were attacked by 200 state troopers and deputies.

9. They were protected by soldiers on the 17th.

10. The Voting Rights Act ended most literacy tests and gave the attorney-general the power to appoint voting registrars.

Pain and Trouble in the Late 1960s (page 99)

1. Head Start was a program that helped preschool children.

2. Thurgood Marshall was selected for the Supreme Court.

3. OEO was an acronym for the Office of Economic Opportunity.

4. African-Americans said that whites with money were going to college or Canada, while the poor and minorities went to Vietnam.

5. Huey Newton and Bobby Seale founded the Black Panthers.

6. Eldridge Cleaver later joined the Black Panthers.

7. In the 1970s, the Panthers' projects were school breakfasts and voter registration.

8. The Kerner Commission looked into the causes of riots.

9. Some of the reasons were police practices, unemployment and underemployment, and poor housing.

10. Kerner Commission warning: "Our nation is moving toward two societies, one black, one white—separate but unequal."

African-Americans Move to the City (page 101)

1. Nixon opposed busing to achieve integration.

2. Wallace attacked integration and welfare mothers.

3. The Civil Rights Act of 1968 outlawed various forms of discrimination.

4. When housing in African-American neighborhoods was shown only to African-American couples, it was called steering.

5. The selling of houses at inflated prices was called block busting.

6. When a bank refused to lend to the homebuyers, it was called redlining.

7. White flight was a term for whites leaving the cities and moving to the suburbs.

8. The city that changed the most was Detroit.

9. The city that changed the least was Washington, D.C.

10. The term used is infrastructure.

Rising African-American Influence in Politics (page 103)

1. Adam Clayton Powell chaired the House Committee on Education and Labor.

2. Colin Powell was the first African-American secretary of state.

3. Edward Brooke was the first African-American senator since Reconstruction.

4. Two African-American women who served in Congress: Shirley Chisholm, Barbara Jordan, Carol Mosley Braun (any two).

5. The national security advisor for George W. Bush was Condoleezza Rice.

6. Ron Brown served as national party chairman.

7. Ralph Bunche received the Nobel Peace Prize.

8. Thurgood Marshall and Clarence Thomas served on the Supreme Court.

9. The first African-American governor of Virginia was Douglas Wilder.

10. The Rainbow Coalition was formed by Jesse Jackson.

Sports and Entertainment (page 105)

1. Players on the "dream team" were Michael Jordan and Magic Johnson.

2. Jackie Robinson was voted MVP.

3. Althea Gibson and Arthur Ashe were successful African-American tennis players.

4. Hattie McDaniel won an Oscar.

5. Luther "Bojangles" Robinson often appeared in Shirley Temple movies.

6. Eddie Anderson played Rochester.

7. Some movies were *Raisin in the Sun, Carmen Jones,* and *Glory.* Other movies may be named; answers will vary.

8. *Roots* was written by Alex Haley.

9. The No. 1 TV show was *The Cosby Show.*

10. Harry Belafonte was a famous African-American calypso singer.

Affirmative Action and Busing (page 107)

1. The Department of Labor required affirmative action.

2. The purpose of affirmative action was to give those who had always been at a disadvantage (minorities and women) a chance to catch up.

3. The word "goals" was assumed to mean "quotas."

4. The company must draw up a plan to reach that number.

5. When those who are not chosen for jobs feel that the hiring standards are lower for minorities than for those not in a minority, it is called reverse discrimination.
6. Allan Bakke took his case to court.
7. Most whites moved to the suburbs, so there were few whites with which to integrate in the cities.
8. Louisville, Kentucky, had trouble when it tried busing.
9. Busing created racial tension.
10. He placed the schools under court control.

Colin Powell: Top General and Diplomat (page 109)
1. His parents came from Jamaica.
2. ROTC stands for Reserve Officers Training Corps.
3. Powell served two tours during the Vietnam War.
4. Powell commanded the First Battalion in Korea.
5. President Ronald Reagan appointed Powell as the national security advisor.
6. The chairmanship of the Joint Chiefs of Staff is the military's highest post.
7. Desert Shield and Desert Storm were part of the Persian Gulf War.
8. George H.W. Bush appointed Powell as the chairman of the Joint Chiefs of Staff.
9. Powell was secretary of state during George W. Bush's first term.
10. Powell spoke before the United Nations.

Condoleezza Rice: Political Powerhouse (page 111)
1. She was appointed secretary of state.
2. President George W. Bush appointed Rice his national security advisor.
3. Rice was born in Birmingham, Alabama.
4. It is based on *con dolcezza,* a musical term meaning to play "with sweetness."
5. There was a lot of racial tension in Birmingham during the time of the Civil Rights movement.
6. She became interested in international relations and government at the University of Denver.
7. Rice was George H.W. Bush's top advisor on the Soviet Union.
8. George W. Bush was the governor of Texas.
9. Rice was a symbol of the Bush commitment to women and minorities.
10. She helped develop the strategy for the War on Terror.

Bibliography/Suggestions for Further Reading

There are literally hundreds of books dealing with African-American history, and not all can be listed. For a more complete list, consult *Books in Print, Subject Guide*. The books included are references that teachers may find useful in their own reading, and some older students may be able to read them and find them useful.

General Reference

Bennet, Lerone, Jr. *Before the Mayflower: A History of Black America*. Chicago: Johnson, 1982.

Foner, Jack. *Blacks and the Military in American History*. New York: Praeger, 1974.

Franklin, John Hope and Alfred A. Moss, Jr. *From Slavery to Freedom*. New York: Alfred A. Knopf, 1987.

Hughes, Langston. *Pictorial History of Black Americans*. New York: Crown, 1983.

International Library of Negro Life and History. New York: Publishers Company, Inc., 1968.

Meier, August and Rudwick, *From Plantation to Ghetto*. New York: Hill & Wang, 1970.

Metzler, Milton. *The Black Americans: A History in Their Own Words*. New York: HarperCollins, 1984.

Ploski, Harry and Roscoe Brown. *The Negro Almanac*. New York: Bellwether Publishing Co., 1967.

Quarles, Benjamin. *The Negro in the Making of America*. New York: Macmillan, 1987.

Redding, Saunders. *They Came in Chains*. Philadelphia: Lippincott, 1950.

Smith, Mabel.*The Black American Reference Book*. Englewood Cliffs: Prentice Hall, 1976.

African-American History to 1865

Blassingame, John W. *The Slave Community*. New York: Oxford Univ. Press, 1979.

Botkin, B.A. *Lay My Burden Down*. Athens: Univ. of Georgia Press, 1989.

Buckmaster, Henrietta. *Let My People Go*. [Underground Railroad] Boston: Beacon, 1959.

Cornish, Dudley. *The Sable Arm: Negro Troops in the Union Army*. New York: Norton, 1966.

Douglass, Frederick. *The Life and Times of Frederick Douglass*. New York: Carol Pub. Group, 1984.

George, Carol. *Segregated Sabbaths*. New York: Oxford, 1973.

Great Slave Narratives. Boston: Beacon, 1969.

Gutman, Herbert. *The Black Family in Slavery and Freedom*. New York: Random, 1977.

Katz, William. *The Black West*. Garden City: Doubleday, 1971.

Killens, John. *Great Gittin' Up Morning: The Story of Denmark Vesey*. New York: Shamal Books, 1980.

Litwack, Leon. *North of Slavery*. Chicago: University of Chicago Press, 1965.

Mannix, Daniel. *Black Cargoes: A History of the Atlantic Slave Trade*. New York: Viking, 1962.

McPherson, James M. *Marching Toward Freedom: Blacks in the Civil War*. New York: Facts on File, 1990.

Stampp, Kenneth. *The Peculiar Institution*. New York: Vintage, 1956.

Starobin, Robert S. *Industrial Slavery in the Old South*. New York: Oxford, 1970.

Turner, Nat. *Confessions of Nat Turner*. Salem, NH: Ayer, 1861.

African-American History 1865–1954

Bruce, Philip. *The Plantation Negro as a Freedman*. Williamstown, MA: Corner House, 1970.

Buckmaster, Henrietta. *Freedom Bound*. [Reconstruction] New York: Collier, 1965.

Clark, Kenneth, *Dark Ghetto*. New York: Harper & Row, 1965.

DuBois, W.E.B. *Black Reconstruction in America*. Cleveland: World, 1968.

Garvey, Amy. *Garvey and Garveyism*. New York: Macmillan, 1970.

Litwack, Leon. *Been in the Storm So Long: The Aftermath of Slavery*. New York: Random, 1980.

Myrdal, Gunnar. *An American Dilemma*. New York: Harper & Row, 1962.

Painter, Nell. *Black Migration to Kansas After Reconstruction*. New York: Norton, 1979.

Bibliography/Suggestions for Further Reading (cont.)

Washington, Booker T. *Up from Slavery*. New York: Penguin, 1986.
White, Walter. *Rope and Faggot*. New York: Arno, 1969.
Woodward, C. Vann. *The Strange Career of Jim Crow*. New York: Oxford, 1974.

African-American History 1954–Present

Belfrage, Sally. *Freedom Summer*. Charlottesville: University Press of Virginia, 1990.
Bennett, Lerone, Jr. *What Manner of Man: A Biography of Martin Luther King, Jr.* Chicago: Johnson, 1968.
Blue, Rose and Corinne J. Naden. *Colin Powell: Straight to the Top*. Brookfield, Connecticut: The Millbrook Press, 1991.
Chaplick, Dorothy. *Up with Hope: A Biography of Jesse Jackson*. New York: Macmillan, 1987.
Coulton, Elizabeth. *The [Jesse] Jackson Phenomenon: The Man, the Power, and the Message*. New York: Doubleday, 1989.
Ditchfield, Christin. *Condoleezza Rice: National Security Advisor* (Great Life Stories). New York: Franklin Watts, A Division of Scholastic, Inc., 2003.
Felix, Antonia. *Condi: The Condoleezza Rice Story*. New York: Newmarket Press, 2002.
Finlayson, Reggie. *Colin Powell*. Minneapolis, MN: Lerner Publishing Group, 2004.
Garrow, David. *The Civil Rights Movement in the United States in the 1950s and 1960s*. Brooklyn: Carlson, 1989.
Gentile, Thomas. *March on Washington*. Washington: New Day Publications, 1983.
Graham, Hugh. *Civil Rights Era*. New York: Oxford, 1992.
Haley, Alex. *The Autobiography of Malcolm X*. New York: Ballantine, 1992.
Jakoubek, Robert. *Martin Luther King, Jr.* New York: Chelsea House, 1990.
King, Martin Luther. *Stride Toward Freedom: The Montgomery Story*. San Francisco: Harper: San Francisco, 1987.
King, Mary. *Freedom Song: A Personal Story of the 1960's Civil Rights Movement*. New York: Morrow, 1987.
Patrick, Diane. *Coretta Scott King*. New York: Watts, 1991.
Powell, Colin L. and Joseph E. Persico. *My American Journey: An Autobiography*. New York: Random House, 1995.
Race Relations in the USA. New York: Scribner's, 1970.
Robinson, Jackie and Duckett, Alfred. *Breakthrough in the Big League: The Story of Jackie Robinson*. North Bellmore, NY: Marshall Cavendish, 1991.
Roland, Della. *The Dream of Peaceful Revolution*. Morristown, NJ: Silver Burdett, 1990.
Silberman, Charles. *Crisis in Black and White*. New York: Random, 1964.
Silver, James. *Mississippi: The Closed Society*. San Diego: Harcourt-Brace, 1978.
Wade, Mary Dodson. *Condoleezza Rice: Being the Best*. Minneapolis, MN: Lerner Publishing Group, 2003.
Williams, Juan. *Eyes on the Prize: America's Civil Rights Years, 1954–1965*. New York: Penguin, 1988.